ISAAC ASIMOV

RECOGNITIONS

detective/suspense
Bruce Cassiday, General Editor

Raymond Chandler by Jerry Speir
P. D. James by Norma Siebenheller
John D. MacDonald by David Geherin
Ross MacDonald by Jerry Speir
Dorothy L. Sayers by Dawson Gaillard
Sons of Sam Spade: The Private Eye Novel in the 70s
by David Geherin

science fiction
Tom Staicar, General Editor

Isaac Asimov by Jean Fiedler and Jim Mele
Ray Bradbury by Wayne L. Johnson
Critical Encounters: Writers and Themes in Science Fiction, edited
by Dick Riley
Critical Encounters II: Writers and Themes in Science Fiction,
edited by Tom Staicar
The Feminine Eye: Science Fiction and the Women Who Write It,
edited by Tom Staicar
Frank Herbert by Timothy O'Reilly
Ursula K. LeGuin by Barbara J. Bucknall
Theodore Sturgeon by Lucy Menger

Also of Interest
The Bedside, Bathtub & Armchair Companion to Agatha Christie,
edited by Dick Riley and Pam McAllister
Introduction by Julian Symons

ISAAC ASIMOV

JEAN FIEDLER AND JIM MELE

FREDERICK UNGAR PUBLISHING CO.
New York

Copyright © 1982 by Frederick Ungar Publishing Co., Inc.
Printed in the United States of America

Library of Congress Cataloging in Publication Data

Fiedler, Jean.
  Isaac Asimov.

  (Recognitions)
  Bibliography: p.
  Includes index.
  1. Asimov, Isaac, 1920–   —Criticism and
interpretation. I. Mele, Jim, 1950–   II. Ti-
tle. III. Series.
PS3551.S5Z59   813'.54   81-70122
ISBN 0-8044-2203-6   AACR2
ISBN 0-8044-6147-3 (pbk.)

CONTENTS

PREFACE

In our desire to give a coherent account of Asimov's development as a writer of science fiction, we have chosen in this volume to group his early short stories and novels into three categories: the pioneering robot works, the future histories, and general science fiction stories that have been anthologized.

Asimov's juvenile books, written as a series and intended for a television audience, have been given a chapter of their own. Although his later works—those written after 1959—defy neat categorization, they do share a common concern: the manifestations of intelligence. In the discussion of later works, we have concentrated on what we consider the important aspects in his exploration of this topic.

A word on the mechanics of this volume. In order to make the book as readable as possible, no superscript numbers have been used in the text. All necessary material has been footnoted in the back of the book. The footnotes are identified by the relevant page and by several recognizable words from the text.

We would like to thank Isaac Asimov himself for his accessibility both in print and in person. His two comprehensive volumes of autobiography were especially valuable. Not only did they make our task easier, but they also proved to be a great source of enjoyment.

Special thanks, too, must go to our editor, Dick Riley, who was as astute and helpful as he was patient.

J.F. and J.M.

New York City
November 1981

INTRODUCTION
"Escape into Reality"

Isaac Asimov is often praised for the impressive quantity and variety of his work, and for his obvious and unusual intelligence. Certainly these are praiseworthy attributes, but such criticism obscures his most significant achievements.

Although Asimov has written more than two hundred books, including mysteries, biblical studies, histories, juveniles, and outstanding scientific works for the layperson, his thirty-four science fiction books are the ones that have made him famous.

Other writers may be more strikingly imaginative, but Asimov's subtle creations have succeeded in permeating modern American science fiction. The reason behind this achievement may be that, for Asimov, science fiction serves a social function:

> Science fiction is based on the fact of social change. In a sense, it tries on various changes for size; it tries to penetrate the consequences of this change or that; and in the form of a story, it presents the results to the view of the public, a public that needs more and more to have the possibilities of change pointed out to it before it is disastrously overwhelmed by it.
>
> It is this which has always made it seem rather ironic to me that science fiction is continually lumped under the heading of "escape

literature," and usually as the most extreme kind, in fact. Yet it does not escape into the "isn't" as most fiction does, but into the "just might possibly be." It is an odd form of escape literature that worries its readers with atom bombs, overpopulation, bacterial warfare, trips to the moon, and other such phenomena, decades before the rest of the world had to take up the problems.

No, no, if science fiction escapes, it is an escape into reality.

Asimov began to write in the days when science fiction was published in periodicals such as *Astounding Science Fiction* and *Amazing Stories*, known as "pulps," descriptive of the cheap paper on which they were printed. The bulk of his science fiction, now collected as stories and novels in anthologies, was originally written for the pulp magazines.

When his origins as a pulp writer are considered, one may wonder why Asimov did not fall into the convention of sensationalism and the kind of imaginative straining that was a hallmark of most such stories. But Asimov was a scientist, and even in his earliest attempts at fiction, his interest in science dictated his method. Once he invented his Three Laws of Robotics, for example, he proceeded in story after story to investigate the various ramifications of these laws. His scientific background also provided him with a vast body of accurate information on which he could draw, and what was even more important, it raised two questions: "Is my hypothesis sound? Can the facts support it?"

In his early stories Asimov worked with a single hypothesis; the entire point of the story was to prove that theory. Soon, though, the proof was no longer of prime importance, and other motivations brought a more complex and more human texture to his work; he began to use truly fictional characters and situations to speculate about future worlds, on an emotional level as well as on a scientific or technical one.

Asimov sold his first science fiction story, "Marooned Off

Vesta," in 1938 at the age of eighteen. Twenty-eight years later his Foundation Trilogy was voted the World Science Fiction Convention's prestigious Hugo Award for the best all-time series, confirming his reputation as one of America's leading science fiction writers. He won a second Hugo, as well as the Nebula Award, for *The Gods Themselves*, published in 1972.

The leap from first story to Hugo and Nebula is a long one that spans many early rejections, innumerable revisions, and a great deal of hard work.

Born in Russia in 1920, Isaac Asimov emigrated with his parents to the United States when he was three and seems to have wasted little time in proceeding to become a writer. He was reading before he went to school—learning to read was a process he figured out by himself. By the time he was seven, he had a library card, but this meant that although he could take out two books at a time, only one could be fiction. As a result, he read a great deal of science and history, and his unusually retentive memory and ability for instant recall enabled him to accumulate a storehouse of information.

It was evident very early that the boy was brilliant, and his parents expected top performance from him—a mark of 95 would be treated by his father as a poor grade for a boy capable of achieving 100 percent. Frequently bored in school, Asimov often entertained himself and others by inventing stories, and he began to make up his own stories—verbally at first, and then at the age of eleven he began to write them down. Despite these forays into his imagination during class, Asimov was an outstanding student at Boys' High School in Brooklyn, from which he was graduated at fifteen. He earned a B.S. from Columbia University in 1939, a Master's degree in 1941, and then a Ph.D. in 1948. As he says in his autobiography, the war came along and interrupted his studies for the latter.

His father's candy store played an important role in /

imov's writing career; when he wasn't helping in the store—which he did for many years even into the college days—he had time to read, but his father forbade what he called junk. The candy store sold dime novels, but these were off limits to him. Then one day, a new magazine appeared in the store; it was called *Science Wonder Stories* and because of the fortunate inclusion of the word "science" in the title, the young Asimov was permitted to read what would later come to be called science fiction—stories he devoured eagerly.

Although he always knew that he wanted to write, his expectations were rather modest. He had a college education to complete and a career in chemistry as a goal; writing was merely an amusement, and the most he felt he could hope for was to make some money that would help with his college tuition.

Asimov recalls with gratitude that his father took his literary aspirations seriously enough to buy him his first new typewriter, a Smith Corona portable. The fact that he had written and submitted two stories had made him, in his father's eyes, "a literary man ... who deserved the best."

In 1938 *Astounding Stories* became *Astounding Science Fiction*, and Asimov began to write letters to the magazine, letters that were actually published. Urged by his father to submit a manuscript in person to the editor, John Campbell, he did so, was encouraged by his reception, and began to meet the editor monthly as well as to send him countless stories. These continued to be rejected, but Campbell apparently perceived the young man's eagerness and knew that he would not quit, no matter how many rejections he was handed.

Then in 1938, he sold his first story—not to Campbell but to another magazine, *Amazing Stories*.

For eleven years he continued to sell science fiction to magazines, using the money to further his education—right up through a Ph.D in biochemistry. But he was not yet thinking of himself as primarily a writer. When in 1950 *Pebble in the Sky*, his first novel, was published, he was an associate professor at the Boston University School of Medicine and writing was still an avocation. Yet, as he says, "It was a curious avocation." He had been writing since the age of eleven and surmised that he was "that serious distortion of the human condition—the compulsive writer."

By the end of 1957 Asimov realized that writing was all he really wanted to do. He had begun to write books on straight science and could hardly consider "twoscore books in eight years a mere sideline. Especially since my writing income was now two and one-half times my school income."

In 1958 he abandoned teaching and began to devote himself entirely to writing. "And if I needed anything to tell me that I had made the right decision, it was the feeling of absolute delight that washed over me as I did so."

That delight has apparently never diminished. As he says in the introduction to his hundredth book, *Opus 100*: "I have never quite recovered from the rather incredulous relief I feel that people are willing to pay me for what I write. If they didn't pay me, I would still write, of course, for I wrote for years before it occurred to me to submit anything for publication."

Two volumes of Asimov's autobiography—*In Memory Yet Green* and *In Joy Still Felt*—cover the first fifty-eight years of his life in great detail.

Since becoming a full-time writer, Asimov has had regrettably little time for science fiction. In the years between 1960 and 1981, despite a notoriously prodigious output, he has written only a few commissioned stories and one novel in the science fiction genre.

It is significant that virtually all of Asimov's science fiction is kept in print by his publishers, even stories written over thirty years ago when he was first attempting to find an outlet for his work. Despite his having written little science fiction since 1959, his stories and novels seem only to gain in popularity. Why does his work continue to attract readers when that of so many of his contemporaries has been supplanted by the work of a new generation of science fiction writers?

For us, the answer lies in his development from teenaged pulp magazine contributor to mature novelist. It would be a mistake, however, to equate strict chronological order with development, and in Asimov's case, it would be impossible, since he commonly worked on a number of stories at the same time, some quite minor and others that proved to be classics.

1

PULP WRITER: THE EARLY STORIES

"Mankind will spread through the whole Galaxy. But people will have to live their lives on shipboard until new methods of interstellar travel are developed, so it will be Martians, not planet-bound Earthmen, who will colonize the Universe. That's inevitable. It's got to be. It's the Martian Way."

The Martian Way

Short stories, mostly written before 1957 for the very active pulp magazine market, comprise the bulk of Isaac Asimov's science fiction. By count, seventeen of Asimov's titles are short story collections; of the remaining seventeen, the three books in the Foundation series are collections of pieces published as individual short stories and serialized in *Astounding Science Fiction. Pebble in the Sky* and *The End of Eternity* were intended as lead novelettes for the pulps and later were lengthened into novels, and *Fantastic Voyage* was a novelization of a movie.

Asimov's science fiction output dropped sharply after 1957 as he switched his attention to writing nonfiction. Sputnik One had gone into orbit on October 4, 1957; Asimov says in *Buy Jupiter*, "and in the excitement that followed, I grew very fervent concerning the importance of writing science for the layman. What's more, the publishers were now fiercely interested in it as well, and in no time at all I found that I had been hounded into so many projects that it became difficult and even impossible to find time to work on major science fiction projects, and, alas, it has continued so to the present day."

The early short stories fall into three categories: the robot stories, the future histories, and general science fiction tales, some loosely related, which Asimov has collected in anthologies such as *Earth Is Room Enough, Nightfall and Other Stories, Buy Jupiter,* and *The Early Asimov.*

The most widely anthologized story in this third category is "Nightfall." Although Asimov does not list the story in his top three, most critics and readers consider "Nightfall" to be his best short story, something which may rankle Asimov since it was only his thirteenth published story (written when he was twenty-one).

Astounding Science Fiction editor, John W. Campbell, Jr., suggested the Ralph Waldo Emerson quote that inspired "Nightfall," "a story set on the planet Lagash where at least one of six suns is always shining." Working with a common assumption that religious writings often contain a kernel of truth about actual events in the very distant past, Asimov has the scientists of Lagash predict that this constantly sunlit world is about to be plunged into total darkness. "The Book of Revelations," now only heeded by a small but powerful group called simply the Cult, predicts that every two thousand fifty years "there came *total darkness all over the world.* And then, they say, things like Stars appeared, which robbed men of their souls and left them unreasoning brutes, so that they destroyed the civilization they themselves had built up."

The scientists have discovered that nine previous civilizations were all destroyed by fire when they reached heights comparable to Lagash's present one. Still, the scientists' prediction of darkness and impending doom is given as little credence by the general population as the Cult's mystical prophecies. With total darkness only four hours away, some scientists have gathered to try to observe the phenomenon while others have entered a "Hideaway" where they hope to escape the fires that will inevitably be set by the panicked light-starved populace. Their aim is to preserve some of the knowledge accumulated by this present civilization for the next one in the cycle, thereby speeding up the next civilization's development and perhaps freeing Lagash from the destructive pattern.

Although the scientists believe that they have distilled the "truth" from the Cult's "religio-mystic notions," they have only the vaguest conception of what the Cultists call Stars, assuming that they are a peripheral phenomenon and that darkness alone causes men to become mad.

As with the Three Laws of Robotics that were soon to follow, Asimov takes an isolated formula or quote, which in itself is devoid of obvious story potential, and proceeds to exploit the least obvious implications of the original thought. The quote from Emerson suggested by Campbell and used to open "Nightfall" is: "If the stars should appear one night in a thousand years, how would men believe and adore, and preserve for many generations the remembrance of the city of God?"

Asimov answers Emerson's rhetorical question by saying that men believe with fanaticism, adore with destruction and madness, and preserve the remembrance of the city of God by "the testimony of those least qualified to serve as historians; that is, children and morons."

With only one of six suns left in the sky, the total eclipse that occurs once every 2,049 years begins, swelling the ranks of the Cult with last-minute converts. For the watching scientists, "the tiny bit of encroaching blackness" not only proved their theory but also "magnified itself into the crack of doom."

Within minutes after total darkness occurs, the scientists can already see the far-off city in flames and can begin to feel themselves going mad. But it was not the darkness alone that was driving them insane.

The strength and power of this story lie in Asimov's

imaginative conception of how human beings would react to the revelation of the Universe's vast proportions and their own world's insignificance.

Through the darkness shone the stars. "Not Earth's feeble thirty-six hundred stars visible to the eye; Lagash was in the center of a giant cluster. Thirty thousand mighty suns shone down in a soul-searing splendor that was more frighteningly cold in its awful indifference than the bitter wind that shivered across the cold, horribly bleak world."

With "Nightfall," the young Asimov not only showed editor Campbell what he was capable of, but he also made the transition from pedestrian stories limited in scope to a much broader canvas. For the first time he began to think in terms of the rise and fall of civilizations—a significant concern that would motivate his Foundation Trilogy and the other future histories, as well as find its way into all his novels.

Only three years earlier, in 1938, a jubilant Asimov had sold his first story, "Marooned Off Vesta" to the pulp science fiction magazine, *Amazing Stories*. Following a stock plot, three men are trapped in an orbiting hulk of a wrecked spaceship. After the standard period of despair, one man comes up with a logical solution, and Asimov leaves them as they head towards salvation.

Only two and half years separate this story and "Nightfall." During that time Asimov had been working diligently at his craft and had even written one story, "The Black Friar of the Flame," that foreshadows the inhabited Galaxy of the Foundation Trilogy. While he was working on "Nightfall," however, he was in "happy ignorance that the story I was now writing was in any way different from those I had been writing all along."

Campbell, an astute editor, was not. When Asimov received a check for the story, he called Campbell to say that he had been overpaid. Campbell informed him that the extra payment was a bonus and that "Nightfall" would be a cover story—Asimov's first.

When one considers the relatively brief period between "Marooned Off Vesta" and "Nightfall," it is evident that "Nightfall" represented a real breakthrough—an intuitive grasp of the potential inherent in science fiction. There had been indications for some time that in spite of being a part-time writer, he was, through constant effort, developing fruitful science fiction concepts that would become the main elements in his best work.

Stories like "Robbie," his first robot story, and "The Black Friar of the Flame"—though clearly inferior to his later works—broke ground for his two main science fiction themes. Both written in 1939, each story sets the tone for its successors. Like "Robbie" the positronic robot stories were essentially a series of simply plotted tales revolving around simple characters. "The Black Friar . . ." deals with complex developments on a galactic scale, as does the Foundation Trilogy set in the far future.

Although Asimov has called "The Black Friar . . ." "the most conspicuous failure in the literary portion of my life," he adds, "it has its interesting points." The most ambitious project in those first years, the novelette was his first attempt to write a future history—"a tale about a far future time written as though it were a historical novel."

It was also his first attempt at exploring a populated galaxy—a galaxy where every planet capable of sustaining life has been colonized by intelligent beings. In itself, any of these elements would have represented an advance in his writing. The combination indicates an ambitious vision—a vision that would require greater skill than Asimov then had available.

In a naïve way, "The Black Friar . . ." tries to deal with the emotional forces of mass psychology and religion, the struggle between the Universe's two intelligent forms of life, and space battles of epic proportions. Earth, humanity's cradle, is under the domination of the reptilian Lhasians. As Lhasa prepares to expand its rule to the other worlds inhabited by humans, nationalists on Earth foment a revolution by preaching a religious crusade against the aliens.

During the decade following the breakthrough of "Nightfall," Asimov returned to the themes that he had touched on in "The Black Friar . . ." but with far greater success. In the forties he produced a series of stories that became the Foundation Trilogy, revolving around mass psychology, galactic struggles, and the rise and fall of civilizations.

Psychology in both "The Black Friar . . ." and the Foundation provides a method of controlling masses of people. In the early story, it is simply a tool for inciting crowds to riot and revolt; the entire revolt against the aliens rests on finding the proper leader, the kind of man who can inflame mobs.

By the time of the Foundation, the psychological manipulation of masses of people has become a mathematical science. Rather than control mobs, the Foundation's psychologists predict mass responses and devise strategies for steering these responses toward their own desired ends.

In both, psychology is employed in an effort to save humanity. The science fiction cliché, annihilation by aliens, threatens human existence in "The Black Friar . . ."; a far subtler danger—30,000 years of barbarism—motivates the Foundation's psychologists.

The young Asimov could imagine an entire galaxy in turmoil. The only way he could depict this turmoil was by describing actual space battles. The premise that two intelligent races were fighting for domination of the Galaxy was hardly an original one, even in 1939, and his literal conception of ships fighting in space takes on unintended comic overtones. In these days of laser weapons and orbiting nuclear armaments, the reader can only smile when Asimov's "needle ships" ram the enemy vessels to win a decisive victory.

The Foundation Trilogy represents galactic struggle in a far subtler and more credible manner. There are battles, but for the most part these are mentioned only in passing. Now Asimov is more interested in describing the economic and political forces that seem to be part of all human struggle. These forces provide a far more appropriate motivation for a topic of this scope. They are forces that are clearly in evidence in every historical confrontation between nations, and we have no difficulty imagining them at work on a galactic level.

Although Asimov calls "The Black Friar . . ." and the Foundation Trilogy "future histories," only in the trilogy does one get a sense of historical perspective, the feeling that one is reading about the fall of a civilization and the forces behind that fall.

The forces at work in "The Black Friar . . ." are too simplistic for a history—the question of whether humanity will survive or disappear can be answered by simply determining whether it is militarily superior to its enemies.

The Foundation shows us in great detail the final years of a galactic empire, its slow dissolution, and the early years of a new empire that rises in its place. Of course, "The Black Friar . . ." is only a short story, and the Foundation stretches through three volumes, but even in the Foundation's first chapter (originally written as a short story) Asimov exhibits that open-ended quality that we equate with history. There is no predictable end in sight even when the story is over.

A significant difference between these works and "The Black Friar . . ." was the absence in the later stories of any but human intelligence in the Galaxy. One of the critical points often made about Asimov's science fiction is that he writes about a "human-only Galaxy." The decision to exclude extraterrestrials was not a literary decision; it was a political one. According to Asimov, he found in his working relationship with Campell that his stories about aliens always required revisions that brought them in line with Campbell's views about the superiority of human intelligence over any other form of intelligence.

"I sometimes got the uncomfortable notion," Asimov writes in *The Early Asimov*,

> that this attitude reflected Campbell's feeling on the smaller, Earth scale. He seemed to me to accept the natural superiority of Americans over non-Americans, and he seemed automatically to assume the picture of an American as one who was of northwest European origin.
>
> I cannot say that Campbell was racist in any evil sense of the term. I cannot recall any act of his that could be construed as unkind, and certainly he never, *not once*, made me feel uncomfortable over the fact that I was Jewish. Nevertheless, he did seem to take for granted, somehow, the stereotype of the Nordic white as the true representative of Man the Explorer, Man the Darer, Man the Victor.

Asimov's invention of the human-only Galaxy was an attempt "to avoid a collision with Campbell's views. I did not want to set up a situation in which I would be forced to face the alternatives of adopting Campbell's views when I found them repugnant and failing to sell a story (which I also found repugnant)."

The critical perception that Asimov's science fiction is characterized by this "human-only Galaxy" is not quite accurate. Despite the evidence of the Foundation and his other future histories, he did write a number of stories in his early career dealing with extraterrestrial intelligence that equal and often surpassed human intelligence. These stories, however, were never offered to Campbell for *Astounding Science Fiction*.

His first efforts with aliens—"Homo Sol," "Half-Breed," "The Black Friar . . .," "Blind Alley"—were written before "Nightfall" and are on a par with the other early stories. For ten years Asimov put aside his Lhasian reptiles, creatures with eight-inch probosci, green Venutians, and the breed that is half-Martian/half-human, while he worked on the Foundation and robot stories. When in the early 1950s he returned to the subject of alien intelligence, it was with far greater imagination and sophistication.

In "Green Patches" the aliens, or more precisely, the alien, is a unified organism—each animal, each insect, and even each plant on Saybrook's Planet shares in a single consciousness. All animal life is vegetarian, and all plants grow replaceable appendages that feed the animals. Nothing appears in overabundance. To the first explorers from Earth, the planet seems like Utopia, except for the disquieting observation that each thing possesses two small patches of green fur.

Unfortunately this unified intelligence has a mania for organization; with a missionary-like zeal born out of pity for the fragmented life forms on Earth, it impregnates every form of female life aboard the spaceship, from white mice to humans. Each fetus has the telltale green patches and has joined the fold of the unified organism.

Before these unified fragments can be transported to Earth where they can carry on the process of salvation, these first explorers recognize the danger and destroy themselves as well as the new converts by blowing up the ship, but not before alerting Earth to the danger of Saybrook's Planet.

When the story begins, this is history and a second expedition is on the planet's surface. Despite extreme precautions, one alien life form, camouflaged as a piece of wire but still bearing the full potential to convert Earth, has managed to get aboard the second spaceship. As the ship takes off for Earth, the wire resists the temptation to immediately begin its work among the fragmented life forms aboard the ship, knowing that it must wait until it reaches Earth to succeed in its mission. Unfortunately it has lodged itself in the ship's hatch mechanism and is electrocuted when the returning explorers arrive home and open the hatch.

The concept of an entire planet possessing one consciousness is not an original one in science fiction. But Asimov succeeds within the confines of the short story in developing both the humorous and dramatic aspects inherent in the situation. Told with low-keyed humor, it is nevertheless a real cliff-hanger with a satisfying solution— one that is integral rather than arbitrary. Although this story probably received no more attention than any of his other stories, "Green Patches" exhibits his imaginative capacity to create extraterrestrial societies that compare favorably with his more famous "human-only" Galaxy.

Four months later he was to write in "Hostess" of very different forms of alien intelligence. Set in the early days of interstellar travel, "Hostess" introduces a representative of one of the Galaxy's four known extraterrestrial intelligences, a doctor from Hawkin's Planet. There are many similarities among all five species, but man is unique in some significant ways—man is carnivorous, the aliens are not; man stops growing early in life, the aliens never stop; man eventually dies, while the aliens live as long as they desire. But perhaps most important, man is immune to Inhibition Death, the mysterious disease that strikes all other forms of intelligence, causing a cessation of growth that leads to involuntary death. The doctor has come to Earth seeking a cure for Inhibition Death which, he feels, lies in understanding man's strange immunity.

Midway through the story the doctor from Hawkin's Planet posits that a sixth intelligence exists—a mysterious mental parasite, the apparent cause of the dread disease. The conclusion most frightening to its earthly hosts is that man is the carrier. As man's interplanetary contacts increase, so will the incidence of Inhibition Death.

The idea of an intelligence that lives as a parasite controlling its hosts despite the lack of its own corporeal body seems a departure for a writer so strongly identified with a "human-only" Galaxy. It is noteworthy not only because it is an *Asimov* alien story, but it also provides new connotations for the concept of intelligence, connotations that would prove to be a major theme in his science fiction of the seventies.

One of the highest functions of science fiction is to speculate on subjects which are usually reserved for scientific philosophers. An excellent example of this kind of speculation, "Hostess" begins with the simple premise that men die and aliens do not. Asimov expands the premise into a convincing case for a most extraordinary life form which not only lives on intelligent mental energies, but also has controlled the evolution of humans since "Adam's fall."

Two other noteworthy speculations among his early stories are "The Deep" and "Each an Explorer." While "The Deep" is not one of his best stories, it presents an original form of alien life that seems to appear again in a more realized and sophisticated form in his finest novel, *The Gods Themselves.*

Both story and novel deal with extraterrestrial societies driven underground by a dying sun, societies that see Earth's energy as their race's salvation. In a general way, both rely on genetic engineering and both use dimensional travel rather than conventional spaceships for their commerce. The main problem with "The Deep" is that it revolves around "mother love," the least interesting aspect of the story and an aspect that arbitrarily pushes it in a direction away from significant science fiction invention.

An even more unusual form of alien life is discovered in "Each an Explorer" although this knowledge is not revealed to the reader until the end of the story.

Two members of Earth's Exploration Teams survey a planetary system that has two inhabitable planets. Because of a malfunction in their spaceship, they are forced to land on one of them and find a rather primitive monkey-like form of life. The local society is a tribal one that seems to revolve around the ritualistic cultivation of a strange plant, unlike any the explorers have ever seen.

Moved by an inexplicable urge to visit the system's other planet, the two Earthmen find a different tribal life form, this one snake-like, tending identical plants. Only when the explorers leave the second planet, do they realize that the truly intelligent life forms are the plants; they deduce that the plants are capable of mind control and that they, the explorers, have been used much like bees to cross-fertilize for genetic vigor.

By inference rather than observation, Asimov's explorers begin finally to paint an accurate picture of the awesome intelligence they have encountered. Since the identical plant forms exist on two planets, they must have been carried from one to the other via space travel. Since it is obvious that even the most intelligent plant cannot negotiate such travel, they had to have been transported by another life form intelligent enough to have mastered space travel. Since the two have had first-hand experience with what Asimov calls the plant's "psionic powers," they deduce that probably one or both of the primitive animal-like forms had at one time been capable of space travel, but since have been totally enslaved by the plants.

Relieved over their narrow escape, they head homeward, unmindful of the fact that this alien intelligence—"with the patience of the plant (the all-conquering patience no animal can ever know)"—has discovered still another civilization temporarily capable of space travel.

Although these alien stories have not achieved the recognition of "The Martian Way" or "Nightfall," they are more than historical curiosities.

Asimov uses these alien stories to conjecture about the true nature of intelligence, often embodying it in forms that fail all man's standard tests for determining intelligence—speech and the manufacture and use of tools. In "Each an Explorer" Asimov endows plants, an organic life form devoid of even a nervous system, with an intelligence superior to man's.

This kind of speculation provides fertile ground for science fiction, and although Asimov's output declined sharply in later years, these early concepts continued to pique his curiosity, coming to elegant fruition in "The Bicentennial Man" and *The Gods Themselves*.

"Sucker Bait," a novelette published in *Astounding Science Fiction*, brings us back to the "human-only Galaxy" that Asimov favored when writing for Campbell. The planet, Troas, seems a perfect candidate for colonization except for one thing: a century earlier over a thousand colonists had died mysteriously after two years of peaceful life on the planet. An expedition composed of physicists, botanists, astronomers, and other specialists has as its mission to learn the cause of these deaths. Among all these specialists is one dedicated generalist—a member of the little-known Mnemonic Service. Where the others are interested in facts pertinent only to their specialty, Mnemonic Mark Annuncio has memorized everything that has passed in front of his eyes since the age of five, his sole motive having been unfocused curiosity. His function is to do the one thing that computers cannot—to approach mountains of information, discover connections that may cross many areas of specialization, and to make the intuitive correlation between these seemingly unrelated facts that renders them usable.

To Annuncio, the minds of the specialists seem like "dusty lumberyards with splintery slats of wood tumbled every which way; and only whatever happened to be on top could be reached." His fellow expedition members, however, see little value in the young Mnemonic's "parroting of facts" and are irritated by his interdisciplinary curiosity.

It is, of course, this unfocused curiosity that enables Mark to unravel the deadly mystery of Troas and to save the present expedition from the fate of its predecessors.

Customarily Asimov employs a directness in his plots which sometimes seems almost abrupt. In "Sucker Bait" he spends a great deal of time describing the planet and its two suns even though this incidental information has little bearing on the plot. As in "Nightfall" and later in *The Caves of Steel*, Asimov is responding to the challenge of writing a story based on an editor's idea. In the case of "Sucker Bait," Asimov, Poul Anderson, and Virginia Blish were each asked to write a story about a planet with two suns, all to be published in a single volume by a small publishing company. The descriptive passages fulfill Asimov's obligation, but the central thesis of the story has nothing to do with a planet illuminated by two suns. Rather he is speculating on the human capability to integrate and manipulate an ever-increasing body of information. Since the beginning of the twentieth century, the response to this information explosion has been specialization, a trend witnessed by Asimov during his years as a research assistant.

In "Sucker Bait," Asimov envisions a future where specialists have so narrowed their perspective that they are totally unable to see beyond their own area of expertise. While admitting the superiority of computers for storage and retrieval, he illustrates the unique human capacity for associative thinking—a capacity that is so crucial to that intuitive leap that leads to the solution of what seems to be a paradox.

When Asimov began to write "The Martian Way" in 1952, Senator Joseph McCarthy and his Committee on Un-American Activities were terrorizing both business and government with accusations of disloyalty. Most terrifying was the fact that in the beginning no one could effectively stop them. Sickened by this "simple-minded and destructive 'patriotism'," Asimov planned to make "The Martian Way" an allegorical commentary on McCarthyism.

Although the narrowness of a McCarthy-like vision is important throughout the story, this is not the element that accounts for its long-standing popularity. By the time it was completed, even Asimov recognized that the story had evolved beyond a simple political allegory; he changed the title from "A Piece of Ocean" to one that reflected the story's true emphasis on a new social order.

A colony on Mars is made up of humans who, after three generations, have adapted to the rigorous demands of life in space. Unlike their Earthbound counterparts, the Martians are able to endure the long periods of confinement necessary for space voyages beyond the near planets, and ultimately they will be the ones to colonize the universe. When the story opens, the Martian colony is still dependent on Earth for its food, and more important, for its water. As Asimov envisioned it in 1952, water was not only essential for life, but steam-propelled all space vehicles. When the Martians are cut off from their supply of Earth water by a McCarthy-like demagogue, the "Martian" way enables them to seek new sources of water in the asteroid belts of deep space, a journey beyond the capacities of people born on Earth.

Although steam has yet to be used to propel spaceships, Asimov is far more accurate in predicting the overall forces that will shape society in the future. Most science fiction writers of that era saw no end to continued expansion fueled by unlimited cheap natural resources. In "The Martian Way," however, Asimov predicts that human society will be shaped by the *scarcity* of cheap resources, a hypothesis that has been sharply underscored by the events of the 1970s.

Based on their observations of the societies in which they lived, the most imaginative writers have been able to project the direction of future societies. Aldous Huxley understood the principle of instant gratification and came up with "Soma." George Orwell was able to envision the growth of totalitarian societies and a corresponding decrease in the individual's rights and importance. Compared to other science fiction writers of the fifties, Asimov has seemed rather conservative in his views of the future, but "The Martian Way" is concrete evidence of his perceptiveness. Writing in a period when the United States was caught up in the idea of unlimited expansion, he was able to see well beyond the post-war euphoria.

This perception of the future was to become the mainstay of Asimov's fiction. Taken as a whole, the early short stories show clearly Asimov's movement towards what he would later call "social science fiction." In the earliest stories like "Marooned Off Vesta" Asimov was writing the kind of adventure story that characterized the science fiction of the period. Within a short time he began to write stories that were "concerned with the impact of scientific advance upon human beings." Asimov came to feel that while some science fiction is primarily concerned with adventure and the hardware of the future, "social science fiction is the only branch of science fiction that is sociologically significant, and that those stories, which are generally accepted as science fiction . . . are not significant, however amusing they may be and however excellent as pieces of fiction."

For Asimov scientific advance has never been the creation of futuristic hardware. Although he invents spaceships propelled by something called hyperdrive and gadgets with names like Atomo-light and Delta-ray gun, he writes about the wider impact of science, a science which is just beginning to open the universe for us; he asks us to relinquish our narrow vision of the world that exists within the boundaries of what we know and to see Earth from the perspective of its place within an almost infinite universe.

"Nightfall" shows us a people so ignorant of the universe's magnitude that they are driven mad when confronted with it. The reader's first reaction is a kind of condescending incredulity at such provincialism. But Asimov's revelation cuts deeper—our own provincialism is exposed. We are forced to consider the implications of all those stars shining in *our* sky.

Asimov himself defines science fiction as "that branch of literature which deals with the response of human beings to advances in science and technology." It must, he claims, be "based on the fact of social change.... In a sense, it tries on various changes for size; it tries to penetrate the consequences of this change or that; and, in the form of a story, it presents the results to the view of the public, a public that needs more and more to have the possibilities of change pointed out to it before it is disastrously overwhelmed by it."

The main point of "Nightfall" is that we must be open to new conceptions of ourselves and our place in an unbounded world. In stories such as "The Black Friar of the Flame" and "The Martian Way" Asimov gives us a picture of the world as boundaries fade and change.

"The Martian Way" is a good example of a problem that defies solution until people perceive that science has subtly changed them. Only when they become aware that, although still human, they are *Martians* and no longer bound by the rules and restrictions of life on Earth, do they see Mars for what it really is: not an outpost of Earth, but the first step towards colonizing the universe.

The effects of science on the physical world around us are apparent. The automobile, the airplane, and television remind us that science has given us things our ancestors never had. We are aware that our science has and is changing the face of the Earth, but what is far less obvious are the ways in which we are changing. The Martians point proudly to the ways in which they have altered Mars and made it habitable. For Asimov, what is important is that the colonists finally realized how greatly Mars has changed them. Their salvation in this optimistic story lies in this recognition.

Even in his early story "The Black Friar of the Flame," Asimov attempts to take a common perception and to examine it from a new perspective. It is a widely held belief that through science we will eradicate disease, poverty, and discontent, and "build a better world."

"The Black Friar . . . ," however, paints a darker picture of scientific progress. Science has opened the Galaxy to mankind and provided it with universal comfort and prosperity. But instead of creating an Eden, it has helped to create the conditions for humanity's extinction. Their physical well-being insured, the great majority of people have lost a spiritual quality—unwilling to risk the loss of physical comfort, they accept domination by an alien power. Only a handful of rebels recognize that a subtle but dangerous apathy has accompanied this scientific progress.

Apathy is not the problem in "Sucker Bait." Here scientific curiosity has motivated human beings into far-reaching, often dangerous, explorations. But in their zeal scientists have pursued specialization to the point that no one person is capable of an overall understanding of a complex problem. Although the exploration team in this story includes among others an astrophysicist, a geochemist, and a microbiologist, one of the characters explains: "Not one of us knows exactly which of our own data is meaningful to the other under a given set of circumstances."

The danger is that few scientists even realize the degree of isolation to which their specialization has led them. The problem they are faced with in this story does not resist solution merely because of its complexity. By projection, Asimov implies that this type of compartmentalized knowledge can only lead to a stasis in human development.

Even concepts as commonplace as intelligence and death yield to Asimov's vision of change.

Human extinction is often the threat in Asimov's stories, and just as often the threat arises from our inability to shake preconceived notions, to change our perceptions as science extends our reach. Explorers surveying distant planets plant the seeds for human extinction in "Each an Explorer" because they cannot fathom, until it is too late, that intelligence is not limited to animal life. They assume, in the face of all evidence, that the primitive animals they observe tending plants control two adjacent planets. Only when they are headed towards Earth do they perceive that the plants are the dominant intelligent life form; even then they fail to see that they are under the plants' power carrying seeds back to Earth.

"Green Patches" considers intelligence from still another perspective—the unified organism with many parts sharing one consciousness. Here men do recognize the nature of the intelligence they are dealing with, yet their preconceptions blind them to the unlikely forms that this intelligence can assume. Once again lack of vision creates a threat to humanity, one that humanity escapes only through blind luck.

In one of his most interesting early stories, "Hostess," Asimov takes a startling view of intelligence, connecting it with death. Man dies only because of the existence of mental parasites, members of an intelligent race that remains undiscovered until an alien observer deduces its presence. Men and women have played host to this parasite since "Adam's fall." Able to imagine alien races inhabiting distant planets, they cannot conceive of one inhabiting their minds.

The strength of these early stories lies in Asimov's ability to take the commonplace, the ordinary, and say, "Look again." He claims that he wanted to prepare his readers for change. To accomplish this he emulated the best writers by reinventing the world for us, by observing Ezra Pound's dictum "Make it new." Asimov chose to base his reinvention on science, to take a scientific perspective that threatens to dwarf us and reveal the human element that makes it truly new.

After more than ten years of publishing science fiction stories in pulp magazines like *Astounding Science Fiction*, Asimov published in 1950 his first full-length novel, *Pebble in the Sky*. By the end of that decade he had published fifteen novels, including some of his most successful. In 1954, however, he turned the larger portion of his attention to popular science writing, and his short science fiction output declined drastically; he published few new stories in the latter part of the decade. Still, his reputation as a science fiction writer continued to grow, due in large part to these early short stories which were made available in collections issued by his publishers—*I, Robot, The Martian Way and Other Stories, Earth Is Room Enough*, and *Nine Tomorrows*. In fact, Asimov had written so prolifically between 1939 and 1954, years when his primary output consisted of short stories, that collections of these early stories continued to appear and reach new generations of readers throughout the next two decades.

2

A NEW KIND OF MACHINE: THE ROBOT STORIES

"There was a time when humanity faced the universe alone and without a friend. Now he has creatures to help him; stronger creatures than himself, more faithful, more useful, and absolutely devoted to him. Mankind is no longer alone."

I, Robot

Of all his creations, Asimov himself says, "If in future years, I am to be remembered at all, it will be for (the) three laws of robotics."

These three laws, deceptively simple at first glance, have led to a body of work—twenty-two short stories, two novels, one novella—that has permanently changed the nature of robots in science fiction. Far from confining Asimov, these laws sparked his imagination, provoking inventive speculation on a future technology and its effect on humanity.

As a science fiction reader in the thirties, Asimov says he resented the Frankenstein concept, then rampant in science fiction, of the mechanical man that ultimately destroys its master. Annoyed with what he perceived as a purely Faustian interpretation of science, early in his career he decided to try his hand at writing stories about a new kind of robot, "machines designed by engineers, not pseudo men created by blasphemers."

"Robbie," his first robot story, published in 1940 unveils a machine with a "rational brain," a machine created solely for the use of mankind and equipped with three immutable laws which it cannot violate without destroying itself.

These laws, essential to Asimov's conception of the new robot, he dubbed the Three Laws of Robotics: First Law— A robot may not injure a human being or through inaction allow a human being to come to harm; Second Law—A robot must obey the orders given it by human beings except where such orders would conflict with the First Law; Third Law—A robot must protect its own existence as long as such protection does not conflict with the First and Second Laws.

Despite their apparent simplicity these laws are among Asimov's most significant contributions to a new kind of science fiction. Using the Three Laws as the premise for all robotic action, he proceeded to write a series of stories and later two novels that presented the relationship of technology and humanity in a new light.

When "Robbie" first appeared in *Super Science Stories,* it is unlikely that any reader would have been able to discern the truly revolutionary nature of this elementary robot. "Robbie" is an uncomplicated, even naive story of a nonvocal robot who was built to be a nursemaid. From the beginning, Asimov wages his own war on the Frankenstein image of the new robot. Gloria, the child, loves Robbie as a companion and playmate. Her mother, Grace Weston, dislikes and distrusts the robot, whereas her father, George Weston, acknowledges the Three Laws of Robotics and sees the robot as a useful tool that can never harm his child.

In spite of wooden characters and a predictable plot, this early robot story is the first step in Asimov's investigation of the potential inherent in the Three Laws and the, as yet unforeseen, ramifications of his new robotic premise.

In the stories that followed "Robbie," it seems clear that Asimov's scientific background suggested a technique that he could use to investigate and exploit this new character, the non-Frankenstein robot. Like a scientist working in the controlled environment of a laboratory, Asimov took the Three Laws as an inviolate constant and logically manipulated them to produce unforeseen results, expanding his robotic characters and his own fiction-making ability along the way.

In a sense the Three Laws *are* the plot in Asimov's early robot stories. By allowing the actions of the various robots seemingly to contradict one of the laws, Asimov creates tension which he then releases by letting his human characters discover a logical explanation, that is, one that works within the framework of the robotic laws.

This is the real difference between the Robot stories and the Foundation series that he was working on at the same time. In the latter he writes as a historian paralleling Gibbon's *Decline and Fall of the Roman Empire*. The stories are sequential, each new story building on its predecessors to present an historical context. He was able to develop the Robot stories in a very different manner, free to add new elements without regard for temporal continuity.

Using his formula, Asimov followed "Robbie" with eleven more robot stories, all published in various science fiction pulp magazines, the best of which were collected under the title, *I, Robot* and published by Gnome Press in 1950.

In the *I, Robot* stories, Asimov introduces three central human characters to link the stories together as well as bringing in a number of concepts that quickly become central to this expanding robotic world. Susan Calvin, a robot psychologist or roboticist, is the main character in some stories. She has an intuitive, almost uncanny understanding of the thought processes of Asimov's peculiar robots. When the stories leave the Earth's surface, two new characters take over—Gregory Powell and Mike Donovan, troubleshooters who field-test new robots. Susan Calvin remains behind to record their exploits for curious reporters and historians. All three are employees of U.S. Robots and Mechanical Men, the sole manufacturers of Asimovian robots.

By the second story in *I, Robot*, "Runaround," Asimov has invented a name for the phenomenon that sets his robots apart from all their predecessors—the positronic brain, a "brain of platinum-iridium sponge . . . (with) the 'brain paths' . . . marked out by the production and destruction of positrons." While Asimov has readily admitted, "I don't know how it's done," one fact quickly becomes clear—his positronic brain gives all of his robots a uniquely human cast.

In "Runaround" Powell and Donovan have been sent to Mercury to report on the advisability of reopening the Sunside Mining Station with robots. Trouble develops when Speedy (SPD-13), who has been designed specifically for Mercury's environs is sent on a simple mission essential both to the success of the expedition and to their own survival.

Instead of heading straight for the designated target, a pool of selenium, Speedy begins to circle the pool, spouting lines from Gilbert and Sullivan, and challenging Powell and Donovan to a game of catch.

At first glance it seems that Speedy is drunk. However, never doubting that the Three Laws continue to govern the robot's behavior, as bizarre as it is, the two men proceed to test one hypothesis after another until ultimately they hit upon a theory that explains Speedy's ludicrous antics and "saves the day."

"Reason" presents the two engineers with an unexpectedly complex robot, the first one who has ever displayed curiosity about its own existence. Cutie (QT-1) has been built to replace human executives on a distant space station which beams solar energy back to Earth. A skeptic, Cutie cannot accept Powell's explanation of the space station's purpose. Instead, he develops his own "logical" conception of a universe that does not include Earth, human creatures, or anything beyond the space station.

Beginning with the assumption, "I, myself, exist because I think," Cutie deduces that the generator of the space station is "The Master," that he, QT-1, is his prophet, and that Donovan and Powell are inferior stopgap creations that preceded him.

He tells the two that their arguments have no basis while his are founded on Truth, "Because I, a reasoning being, am capable of deducing Truth from *a priori* Causes. You, being intelligent, but unreasoning, need an explanation of existence *supplied* to you, and this the Master did. That he supplied you with these laughable ideas of far-off worlds and peoples is, no doubt, for the best. Your minds are probably too coarsely grained for absolute Truth."

Although in the end Asimov still uses the Laws to explain Cutie's behavior, for the first time the robot is no longer merely a device to illustrate the workings of his Three Laws. It seems apparent that Asimov in his manipulation went a step further in the characterization of this robot. Cutie is not a simple tool; he is curious, intuitive, considerate of his "inferiors," Donovan and Powell, humoring their "misplaced notions," and ultimately but unconsciously fulfilling the requirements of the First Robotic Law—to protect human life.

When Asimov first began to write about robots, he knew what he did *not* want to perpetuate. Now with Cutie's creation, he began to see the real ramifications of robots who must obey the Three Laws. This new technology—robotics—is softened by human moral and ethical qualities.

A robot unintentionally endowed with the ability to read minds is the hero of "Liar." Of course this ability has profound effects on the robot's interpretation of the Three Laws, an interpretation so logical, so simple that it is overlooked by everyone, including the famed robot psychologist, Susan Calvin. Herbie (RB-34) not only reads minds, but he must consider human psychic well-being in all his actions.

One interesting sidelight to "Liar" is an unusual aspect of Herbie's reading habits. Perhaps revealing Asimov-the-scientist's own interest in that logically suspect form, fiction, Herbie turns his nose up at scientific texts:

> "Your science is just a mass of collected data plastered together by make-shift theory—and all so incredibly simple, that it's hardly worth bothering about.
>
> "It's your fiction that interests me. Your studies of the interplay of human motives and emotions . . .
>
> "I see into minds, you see," the robot continued, "and you have no idea how complicated they are. I can't begin to understand everything because my own mind has so little in common with them— but I try, and your novels help."

This cavalier attitude towards the icons of science fiction is common in Asimov's early robot stories, giving them a refreshing humorous character. The vision of Speedy declaiming Gilbert and Sullivan, Cutie teaching subservient robots to "salaam," or Herbie reading romantic prose is an endearing touch that banishes all Frankenstein overtones.

Working within self-imposed limits often gives rise to the temptation to transgress these limits even if briefly. In "Little Lost Rabbit" Asimov succumbs to the temptation to tamper with the First Law. With his background in biblical studies, he inevitably finds that such a transgression of absolute law can only lead to disaster. He creates a robot who, while still forbidden to harm a human being, has no compulsion to prevent through inaction a human from coming to harm. This modification is performed only because of dire need and over the strenuous objections of the roboticists. His forbidden apple tasted, Asimov is content to return to the invariable perimeter of his Three Laws in the rest of the stories.

By the time he gets to "Escape," Asimov has realized that the emotional characteristics of the robotic personality made possible by the injunctions of the Three Laws have become in unexpected ways the robot's greatest strength.

In "Escape," the largest positronic brain ever built (so large that it is housed in a room rather than in a humanoid body) is asked to solve a problem that has already destroyed a purely functional computer. Susan Calvin and the others realize that the problem of developing a hyperspace engine must involve some kind of dilemma that the purely rational computer cannot overcome.

Endowed with the flexibility of a personality, even an elementary personality, the Brain ultimately does solve the problem but not without a curiously human-like reaction. The nub of the problem is that hyperspace travel demands that human life be suspended for a brief period, an unthinkable act expressly forbidden by the First Law. The Brain, although able to see beyond the temporary nature of the death, is unbalanced by the conflict. Whereas a human might go on a drunken binge, the Brain escapes the pressure of his dilemma by seeking refuge in humor and becoming a practical joker. He sends Powell and Donovan off in a spaceship without internal controls, stocked only with milk and beans. He also arranges an interesting diversion for the period of their temporary death—he sends them on an hallucinatory trip to the gates of Hell.

"Evidence" presents a situation in which Stephen Byerley, an unknown, is running for public office, opposed by political forces that accuse him of being a robot, a humanoid robot. The story unfolds logically with the Three Laws brought into play apparently to substantiate the opposition's claim. Waiting for the proper dramatic moment, Byerley disproves the charges by disobeying the First Law. And ultimately with a climax worthy of O. Henry, Susan Calvin confronts Byerley, leaving the reader to wonder, "Is he, or isn't he?"

In a sense this is the most sophisticated story in *I, Robot*. As a scientist accustomed to the sane and ordered world of the laboratory, Asimov's tendency until now has been to tie together all the loose strands. In "Evidence" he leaves his reader guessing, and this looser, more subtle technique makes the story especially memorable.

The final story in the *I, Robot* collection, "The Evitable Conflict," takes place in a world divided into Planetary Regions and controlled by machines. In this story the interpretation of the First Law takes on a dimension so broad that it can in effect be considered almost a nullification of the edict that a machine may not harm a human being. When Susan Calvin is called in by the World Coordinator, the same Stephen Byerley we have met in "Evidence," to help determine why errors were occurring throughout the regions in the world's economy, the indications were that the machines, the result of complicated calculations involving the most complex positronic brain yet, were working imperfectly. All four machines, one handling each of the Planetary Regions, were yielding imperfect results, and Byerley saw that the end of humanity was a frightening consequence. Although these errors have led to only minor economic difficulties, Byerley fears, "such small unbalances in the perfection of our system of supply and demand . . . may be the first step towards the final war."

Calvin, with her intimate knowledge of robot psychology, discerns that the seeming difficulty is due to yet another interpretation of the First Law. In this world of the future, the machines work not for any single human being but for all mankind, so the First Law becomes, "No machine may harm *humanity* or through inaction allow *humanity* to come to harm."

Because economic dislocations would harm humanity and because destruction of the machines would cause economic dislocations, it is up to the machines to preserve themselves for the ultimate good of humanity even if a few individual malcontents are harmed.

Asimov seems to be saying through Susan Calvin that

mankind has never really controlled its future: "It was always at the mercy of economic and sociological forces it did not understand—at the whims of climate and the fortunes of war. Now the machines understand them; and no one can stop them, since the machines will deal with them as they are dealing with the society—having as they do the greatest of weapons at their disposal, the absolute control of the economy."

In our time we have heard the phrase, "The greatest good for the greatest number," and seen sociopolitical systems that supposedly practice it. But men, not machines, have been in control. As Susan Calvin says in the year 2052, "For all time, all conflicts are finally evitable. Only the machines from now on are inevitable."

Perhaps Asimov realized that he had, following his ever logical extensions of the Three Laws, gone the full robotic circle and returned his "new" robots to the Faustian mold. Although benign rulers, these machines were finally beyond their creators' control, a situation just as chilling as Frankenstein destroying its creator and just as certain to strengthen antitechnology arguments.

Having foreseen the awesome possibility, Asimov leaves this machine-controlled world, to return to it only one more time in 1974.

The *I, Robot* collection, one of two books published by Asimov in 1950, was an auspicious debut for a writer whose name would become one of the most widely recognized in contemporary science fiction. As well as reaching a new audience, *I, Robot* quickly came to be considered a classic, a standard against which all other robot tales are measured.

After *I, Robot*, Asimov wrote only one more short robot story—"Satisfaction Guaranteed"—before his first robot novel in 1953. The novel, called *Caves of Steel*, was followed by five more short stories and in 1956 by the final, at least to date, robot novel, *The Naked Sun*.

Including the six short stories and the two novels, as

well as two early stories which predate the Three Laws, the collection *The Rest of the Robots* was issued by Doubleday in 1964. Although not truly "the rest" (Asimov has written at least five later stories), together with *I, Robot*, it forms the major body of Asimov's robot fiction.

While the two novels in *The Rest of the Robots* represent the height of Asimov's robot creations, the quality of the short stories is quite uneven and most seem to have been included only for the sake of historical interest. Three stories, however, "Satisfaction Guaranteed," "Risk," and "Galley Slave" do stand out.

Although not one of Asimov's most elegant stories, "Satisfaction Guaranteed" presents still another unexpected interpretation of the robotic laws.

Tony (TN-3) is a humanoid robot placed as an experiment in the home of Claire Belmont, an insecure, timid woman who feels that she is hindering her husband's career. Hoping to ease the prevalent fear of robots, U.S. Robots has designed Tony as a housekeeper. They hope that if the experiment is successful in the Belmont household, it will lead to the acceptance of robots as household tools.

While Larry Belmont, Claire's husband, is in Washington to arrange for legal government-supervised tests (a simple device on Asimov's part to leave Claire and the robot sequestered together) Claire experiences a variety of emotions ranging from fear to admiration and finally to something akin to love.

In the course of his household duties, Tony recognizes that Claire is suffering psychological harm through her own sense of inadequacy. Broadening the provision of the First Law to include emotional harm, he makes love to her in a situation he contrives to strengthen her self-image.

Despite its lack of subtlety and polish, "Satisfaction Guaranteed" presents a loving, even tender robot that paves the way for Daneel Olivaw, the humanoid robot investigator in the novels.

In "Risk" an experimental spaceship with a robot at the controls is for some unknown reason not functioning as it was designed to do; a disaster of unknown proportions is imminent. While assembled scientists agree that someone or something must board the ship, find out what has gone wrong, and deactivate the ship's hyperdrive, Susan Calvin refuses to send one of her positronic robots and suggests instead a human engineer, Gerald Black, a man who dislikes robots.

Not because of great physical danger but because there is a frightening possibility of brain damage, Black angrily refuses. Despite the danger that Black could return "no more than a hunk of meat who could make [only] crawling motions," Calvin contends that her million-dollar robots are too valuable to risk.

Threatened with court-martial and imprisonment on Mercury, Black finally boards the ship and discovers what went wrong. Returning a hero, Black is enraged that a human could be risked instead of a robot and vows to destroy Calvin and her robots by exposing to the universe the true story of Calvin's machinations.

With a neat twist displaying that Calvin's understanding of humans is as penetrating as her vision of robots, she reveals that she has manipulated Black as adroitly as she does her mechanical men. She chose him for the mission precisely because he disliked robots and "would, therefore, be under no illusion concerning them." He was led to believe that he was expendable because Calvin felt that his anger would override his fear.

Perhaps Asimov was beginning to fear that his readers had grown to accept robots as totally superior to humans, a condition that could only lead to a predictable and constricting science fiction world. Superior robots would, without exception, be expected to solve every problem in every story for their inferior creators. In "Risk," through Susan Calvin he reminds Black and all other myopic humans of the limits of robot intelligence when compared to the boundless capacity of the human mind: "Robots have no ingenuity. Their minds are finite and can be calculated to the last decimal. That, in fact, is my job.

"Now if a robot is given an order, a *precise* order, he can follow it. If the order is not precise, he cannot correct his own mistake without further orders.... 'Find out what's wrong' is not an order you can give to a robot; only to a man. The human brain, so far at least, is beyond calculation."

"Galley Slave," the last short story in *The Rest of the Robots*, marks yet another change in Asimov's attitude towards robot technology.

Easy (EZ-27), a robot designed to perform the mental drudgery that writers and scholars must endure when preparing manuscripts for the printer, is rented by a university to free professors from proofreading galleys and page proofs.

Easy performs his duties perfectly until he makes a number of subtle changes in a sociology text which, strangely enough, was written by the one faculty member opposed to robots.

The changes, undetected until the text has been printed and distributed, destroy the author's career, and the result is a $750,000 suit against U.S. Robots. Susan Calvin, as always, is certain that the errors are the result of human meddling and not robotic malfunction.

In every other case Asimov has chided shortsighted people for refusing to allow robots to free them from menial work. Now as a writer with technology encroaching on his own domain, Asimov's characterization of the antirobot argument is much more sympathetic than ever before.

Explaining his motives to Susan Calvin, the person responsible for Easy's misuse says,

> For two hundred and fifty years, the machine has been replacing Man and destroying the handcraftsman.... A book should take shape in the hands of the writer. One must actually see the chapters

grow and develop. One must work and re-work and watch the changes take place beyond the original concept even. There is taking the galleys in hand and seeing how the sentences look in print and molding them again. There are a hundred contacts between a man and his work at every stage of the game—and the contact itself is pleasurable and repays a man for the work he puts into his creation more than anything else could. *Your robot would take all that away.*

Foreshadowing the two novels, "Galley Slave" reveals an Asimov now wary of overreliance on robotic labor.

3

SCIENCE FICTION MYSTERIES: THE ROBOT NOVELS

"What is beauty, or goodness, or art, or love, or God? We're forever teetering on the brink of the unknowable, and trying to understand what can't be understood. It's what makes us men."

The Caves of Steel

By 1952 Asimov had written four novels, all dealing with only human characters. But in the course of discussing a possible new novel with Horace Gold, his editor at *Galaxy*, Asimov balked when "some sort of robotic plot" was suggested, and objected even more strenuously when his editor mentioned a robot detective. "How," he asked, "can you be fair with the reader if you can at will drag in futuristic devices?" When Gold responded with, "What do you want ... something easy?" Asimov said he had no choice but to get to work. He accepted the challenge of putting together two mass fiction genres and accomplished a fully developed work, *The Caves Of Steel*, that does not violate the spirit of either.

Not one to retire good characters prematurely, Asimov published a second science fiction mystery, *The Naked Sun*, in 1956, reuniting human detective Elijah Baley and his robot partner Daneel Olivaw.

Asimov's basic theme in his short stories—an emotional argument for technology as a useful, practical tool that cannot succeed without human direction—develops new subtlety and strength in the full-length novel *The Caves of Steel*. Here Asimov again uses the Three Laws of Robotics as the premise for all plot action, a technique he perfected in his *I, Robot* stories and one well suited to the deductive reasoning essential to murder mysteries. These Laws offset the use of "futuristic devices" by giving the reader hard and fast rules with which to judge clues, alibis, and the accoutrements of a mystery.

Set 2,000 years in the future, *The Caves of Steel* presents contrasting pictures of Earth and the Outer Worlds—colonized planets throughout the Galaxy. Although the inhabitants of the Outer Worlds trace their origins to Earth, they are separated from it by much more than mere distance, now calling themselves Spacers and ruling the decaying mother planet as benevolent despots. Earth, as antitechnology as it can afford to be, has developed a fragile society torn apart by rioting and dissension. In contrast, the Outer Worlds' total reliance on technology, especially robots, has created stable but stagnant societies peopled by strong individuals with equally strong materialistic appetites.

On Elijah Baley's Earth eight billion people live in eight hundred Cities. "Each City . . . a semiautonomous unit, economically all but self-sufficient. It could roof itself in, gird itself about, burrow itself under. It became a steel cave, a tremendous self-contained cave of steel and concrete."

The close quarters, as well as strained food and energy production systems, have produced a communal, though stratified, society which adopts a name first coined in the French Revolution—civism. People eat in common kitchens, utilize communal bathrooms called personals, watch communal television. Privileges ranging from a seat on the expressways to a private office with a window separate the various strata of the society, strata patterned after present-day civil service ranks.

Elijah Baley, a plainclothesman in the New York City Police Force, has reached the C-5 level, entitling him to a seat on the expressways during nonrush hours, a railing around his desk at work, a three-room apartment with a private wash basin, and three meals a week in his own kitchen with his wife Jessie and their son.

This secure little world is shaken when Baley is asked to investigate the murder of a Spacer scientist, a member of that elite Outer World compound on Earth called Spacetown.

Not only does the murder of a Spacer by an Earthman present grave danger of retribution to the vulnerable Earth, but Baley is forced to take on as a partner a Spacer robot, R. Daneel Olivaw. Since most humans on Earth are as violently antirobot as they are anti-Spacer, Baley views this assignment with distaste, though he is forced to accept it.

Before this first robot novel, Asimov's robot characters are developed at the expense of their flesh and blood counterparts. Traditionally science fiction and, to a lesser extent, mystery have been long on story, short on characterization, and in this series Asimov, except for a few memorable robots in the short stories, follows in the tradition. However when he sets himself the problem of this new form, the mystery science fiction novel, his priorities of necessity shift, and Baley becomes as rounded and developed a human character as Joseph Schwartz in *Pebble in the Sky* and the Mule in the Foundation series. At the same time, Asimov's main robot character gains a new depth when teamed up with a well-portrayed human partner.

Once Asimov gets beyond Baley and Daneel, however, he tends to see his other characters merely as cogs in the wheels of his plot. As a result, Chief of Police Enderby, Jessie and Baley's son Bentley fill the immediate needs of the plot but never really come alive.

He gives Jessie one strong characteristic, a romantic identification with her biblical name Jezebel, but only because the characteristic is essential to the plot.

Enderby's sentimental attachment to bygone ways and customs—archaic affectations like eyeglasses and windows in his office—primarily serve not to flesh out a character but as clues to the ultimate solution of the plot.

Despite thin secondary characters, Asimov's storytelling technique is so compelling that it more than compensates for any flaws. This storytelling faculty is further enhanced by his ability to convincingly illustrate his belief in a humanistic technology, typified by positronic robots, without disrupting his narrative with sermons.

When he is freed from the confining boundaries of the short story, Asimov's descriptive style also improves in both technique and drama. The science fiction writer must create a vision of worlds that do not exist. In *The Caves of Steel* Asimov's inner vision of a future Earth is so clear that his descriptions are vivid, tight, and evocative.

His introduction to the City, for example, is a well-crafted combination of simile and carefully chosen sensory details:

> There were the infinite lights; the luminous walls and ceilings that seemed to drip cool, even phosphorescence; the flashing advertisements screaming for attention; the harsh steady gleam of the "lightworms" that directed THIS WAY TO JERSEY SECTIONS FOLLOW ARROWS TO EAST RIVER SHUTTLE, UPPER LEVEL FOR ALL WAYS TO LONG ISLAND SECTIONS.
>
> Most of all there was the noise that was inseparable from life: the sound of millions talking, laughing, coughing, calling, humming, breathing.
>
> "No directions anywhere to Spacetown," thought Baley.
>
> He stepped from strip to strip with the ease of a lifetime's practice. Children learned to "hop the strips" as soon as they learned to walk. Baley scarcely felt the jerk of acceleration as his velocity increased with each step. He was not even aware that he leaned forward against the force. In thirty seconds he had reached the final sixty-mile-an-hour strip and could step aboard the railed and glassed-in moving platform that was the expressway.

In his earlier novels, Asimov mastered the translation of speech into its written equivalent; but to recreate the speech of a human being is a problem every novelist faces. Credible robotic speech is a much less common challenge, and in *The Caves of Steel* Asimov has developed a form of dialogue for Daneel that is completely believable. Daneel's speech, while possessing the rather formal lilt one might expect from a machine, also possesses a gentle, tempered quality that allows him to pass for human. Only because Baley has been expecting a robot partner does he realize that he is being informed by a machine: ". . . it is customary on my world for partners to call one another by the familiar name. I trust that that is not counter to your own customs." The reader, too, is always conscious of a slight mechanical flavor; still, it is quite believable that no uninformed human being would ever suspect that Daneel is anything but human. Even Daneel's name, the result, Asimov says, of a typographical error, mirrors his slightly skewed human speech.

What made it possible for Asimov to extend his robot stories to this novel length was the mystery element. Because his Three Laws of Robotics give the reader an absolute framework for judging actions and motives, he was able to blend mystery and science fiction, something he had been skeptical of accomplishing.

The universality of the laws allows Baley to consider various hypotheses in a future world without an unfair advantage over the twentieth-century reader. When Baley considers the possibilities that robots were involved in the murder, armchair detectives can draw their own conclusions.

In turn, this longer form allows Asimov to exploit fully his thesis: if humanity is to survive, it must overcome its fear of technology and learn to become its master.

As the novel draws to an end, Baley expresses an almost missionary zeal in his attempt to pass on to the antirobot forces what he has learned:

> "What are we afraid of in robots? If you want my guess, it's a sense of inferiority. . . . They seem better than us—only they're not. That's the damned irony of it."

Baley felt his blood heating as he spoke. "Look at this Daneel I've been with for over two days. He's taller than I am, stronger, handsomer. . . . He's got a better memory and knows more facts. He doesn't have to sleep or eat. He's not troubled by sickness or panic or love or guilt.

"But he's a machine. I can do anything I want to him, the way I can to that microbalance right there. . . .

"We can't ever build a robot that will be even as good as a human being in anything that counts, let alone better. We can't create a robot with a sense of beauty or a sense of ethics or a sense of religion. There's no way we can raise a positronic brain one inch above the level of perfect materialism.

"We can't, damn it, we can't. Not as long as we don't understand what makes our own brains tick. Not as long as things exist that science can't measure. What *is* beauty, or goodness, or art, or love, or God? We're forever teetering on the brink of the unknowable, and trying to understand what can't be understood. It's what makes us men."

It is a persuasive argument, one that Asimov carefully highlights in his logical evolution of a robot-based technology in the year 4000. This close attention to the future technology as well as to the formulation of an equally logical mystery may account for some flaws in his creation of a future society.

Increased population in the forty-first century has created social and economic pressures that have led to such devices as communal kitchens and bathrooms in crowded underground Cities. It seems unlikely that the nuclear family would have survived in this climate. Yet Elijah Baley is married in the twentieth-century connotation of the word to Jessie, and together with their son they live a normal nuclear family life: Baley works, Jessie keeps house, Bentley goes to school, and they all live together in their three-room apartment.

Asimov predicts radical changes in the hardware of human life. Yet he did not consider the possibility of a human revolution that was only a decade away. Jessie is a 1940-vintage domestic woman, as are her women friends; only white people are visible on this Earth.

In the final analysis, however, *The Caves of Steel* easily rises above its shortcomings. Elijah Baley and Daneel Olivaw develop a strong relationship that sustains both the mystery plot and the science fiction premise. This relationship, unequaled in Asimov's work until he produced *The Gods Themselves* eighteen years later, is so intriguing and has so much vitality that it is a natural for a sequel.

And so when *The Naked Sun* was released in 1956 an eager audience awaited the Baley/Daneel reunion. Baley himself was hardly displeased at the resumption of their partnership, in sharp contrast to his original objections in *The Caves of Steel*.

Baley has been sent to Solaria, one of the Outer Worlds, to investigate a murder. This is a highly unusual event in the forty-first century—no Earthman has ever been allowed to visit the Outer Worlds and Earth's leaders suspect intrigue on a galactic scale.

Solaria is a large planet inhabited by only 20,000 people, a wealthy planet virtually without crime and without a police force. Baley, recommended by the Spacers he worked with in *The Caves of Steel*, panics at the idea of even leaving his City, let alone traveling in space to a distant planet. Agoraphobia is a malady common to all inhabitants of Earth and its closed Cities. Only Earth's dire political situation as the weakest member of the Galaxy and its desperate need for first-hand information about the Outer Worlds provide the leverage that gets Baley aboard the Spacers' hyperspace craft.

As the spaceship lands on Solaria, Baley is losing the battle against his open-space phobia and waits uneasily for an unnamed Spacer partner. When Daneel walked in, "He had an almost unbearable desire to rush to the Spacer and embrace him, to hug him wildly, and laugh and pound his back and do all the foolish things old friends did when meeting once again after a separation."

Baley quickly finds that this Outer World is the exact opposite of Earth. Eight billion Earthlings live in crowded, dense Cities while Solarians live on 10,000-acre estates and find even the physical presence of a mate repugnant. With 10,000 robots for every human on the planet, Solaria possesses the most advanced robot economy in the universe, and Solarians all belong to a leisure class supported by two hundred million laboring robots. To Baley, it seems that "an observer from without might think Solaria a world of robots all together and fail to notice the thin human leaven."

Solaria's problems, too, are the exact opposite of those plaguing Earth. In *The Caves of Steel*, Earth is depicted on the verge of total destruction because of its antipathy to robots, that is, to modern technology. Solaria is faced with a destruction not as immediate but just as certain, as humans abrogate almost all responsibility by accepting the unquestioned supremacy of technology.

Echoing this prediction on a narrower, more personal level, *The Naked Sun* also shows that no matter how benign the technology and no matter what the internal safeguards, it will be used for illicit purposes by some. Technology is an ambiguous blessing, no matter who or what controls it.

This is a perception Asimov seemed to gain as he wrote about and considered the many undesirable permutations of robotic action possible within the constrictions of the Three Laws. There are sixteen years between "Robbie" and *The Naked Sun*. While the essential character of robots has not changed drastically, compare the world of Robbie to Solaria. Even if there were two hundred million nursemaids like Robbie, Asimov would never have portrayed this as a detriment to society.

In 1940, Asimov's blind faith in technology as a cure-all mirrored an almost national religious fervor. After sixteen years of writing about robots, although far from disenchanted, Asimov was admitting that technological development had serious dangers.

An important murder investigation is forcefully taken out

of the hands of Solarian officials by Elijah Baley. Despite his feelings of inadequacy—Spacers have long been considered the superior beings of the Galaxy—Plainclothesman Baley is a natural leader on this planet largely because he comes from a world that has refused to accept the axiom, "A robot can do it better." Even Daneel, who shared the spotlight with Baley in *The Caves of Steel*, is now eclipsed.

Too, as representative of the human ethic, Baley commands more of Asimov's attention than in the earlier novel. He shows us the interior Baley, exploring and probing his phobias, his desires until now largely unexpressed, and his internal strengths. Even his superiority over Daneel is more pronounced. Convinced that Daneel is merely an exceedingly useful tool, Baley no longer needs to twit him about only being a robot and even experiences twinges of guilt rather than a sense of accomplishment at having bested a robot when he has Daneel imprisoned. In fact he is now more assured in his dealing with all robots, able to use or not use them as reason dictates.

Concurrently, robots are so well integrated into Asimov's own mythology that they no longer command the reader's attention as a novelty. Unencumbered by the pressures of stardom, Daneel has been freed to illustrate an exemplary robotic nature, a nature that highlights the positive aspects of advanced technology.

Not only have Baley and Daneel evolved for the better, but the minor characters, too, have been developed more adeptly.

While his female characters, Gladia Delmarre and Klorissa Cantoro, are still cast in stereotype "feminine" molds, Asimov displays much more interest in endowing both with individual personality traits for the sake of lending depth to the characters. In obvious contrast, all of Jessie's actions and motives are directly related to plot in *The Caves of Steel*.

Gladia, prime suspect and wife of the murdered man, is

a sensuous woman in the tradition of Hester Prynne, the temptress who is "plagued" by her nature. In her scenes with Baley, there is a strong sense of human interaction, each curious about the other, each probing with cautious discretion. The differences between their home planets, Earth and Solaria, are so great, and yet from the beginning their mutual sympathy is tangible to the reader.

As an Earthman, Baley is terrified of open spaces; as a Solarian, Gladia finds it equally hard to be in the physical presence of another human being. When she finally allows Baley to visit her, she observes,

> ". . . the walls about you. That's what's most in you, the way you can't go outside, the way you have to be inside. You *are* inside there. Don't you see?"
>
> Baley saw and somehow he disapproved. He said, "Those walls aren't permanent. I've been out today."
>
> "You have? Did you mind?"
>
> ". . . The way you mind seeing me. You don't like it but you can stand it."

Asimov, in an apparent decision to add sexual drives to Baley's growing character, also succeeds in imparting an emotional reality well beyond mere desire to this intellectually conceived science fiction world. When Baley and Gladia part, she asks,

> "May I touch you? I'll never see you again, Elijah."
>
> "If you want to."
>
> Step by step, she came closer, her eyes glowing, yet looking apprehensive, too. She stopped three feet away, then slowly, as though in a trance, she began to remove the glove on her right hand. . . .
>
> Her hand was bare. It trembled as she extended it.
>
> And so did Baley's as he took her hand in his.
>
> They remained so for one moment, her hand a shy thing, frightened as it rested in his. He opened his hand and hers escaped, darted suddenly and without warning toward his face until her fingertips rested featherlight upon his cheek for the barest moment.
>
> She said, "Thank you, Elijah. Good-bye."
>
> He said, "Good-bye, Gladia," and watched her leave.

Even the thought that a ship was waiting to take him back to Earth did not wipe out the sense of loss he felt at that moment.

The murdered man's assistant, Klorissa, at first glance seems to be a reincarnation of Susan Calvin, the cold, efficient, superior female scientist. But she, too, quickly rises above the stereotype as she exhibits nuances inherent in dimensional characterization—her aggressiveness is marred by doubt; personal inhibition occasionally disturbs her professional objectivity.

Asimov's skill and perception are extended to a sizable number of other minor characters, allowing him to advance the story smoothly without upsetting the balance between emotion and intellect.

The Naked Sun differs from *The Caves of Steel* in another important respect. Although still supplying the action, the mystery is not nearly so important as Asimov's speculations and conclusions about the future. *The Caves of Steel* is a good mystery set in a believable science fiction world. In *The Naked Sun,* however, the mystery takes a back seat as Asimov places stronger emphasis on the science fiction novel and all the broad connotations implicit in that genre. Once again he was writing "social science fiction," writing about "the response of humans to advances in science and technology." He asks the reader to do more than help to solve a mystery; he asks the reader to join him in speculating about the future of humanity.

This speculation on the evolution of man and his technology is carefully woven into the tapestry of the entire novel, but not until the end does Asimov reveal his overall design. Not until the very end of the novel does he justify the immediate intuitive bond between Baley and Gladia. Both in their own way are able to violate deeply ingrained taboos, are able to perceive the stagnation of their respective societies.

Back on Earth, the murder solved, Baley finally comes to understand that Earth is "Solaria inside out." Solaria has embraced technology, excluding humanity; Earth has worshipped humanity, vilifying technology. Both seemed doomed to eventual extinction.

But Gladia's decision to leave Solaria for a new world and her "courage to face disruption of habits so deeply settled . . . seemed symbolic" to Baley. "It seemed to open the gates of salvation for *us* . . . for all mankind."

Comprehending the symbolic nature of Gladia's act, Baley realizes that he, too, has taken the first steps toward a new world. He "had left the City and could not re-enter. The City was no longer his. . . ." If he could take this step, so would others. Earth would outlive its Caves of Steel.

While Asimov was writing *The Naked Sun*, it became clear to him that what he was working on was the second novel of a trilogy. As he says in his afterword:

> In *The Caves of Steel* I had a society heavily overweighed in favor of humanity. In *The Naked Sun*, on the other hand, I had an almost pure robot society with only a thin leaven of humanity barely holding it together.
>
> What I needed to do next was form the perfect topper to my vision of the future by setting the third novel of the trilogy in Aurora, and depicting the complete fusion of man and robot into a society that was more than both and better than either.

The third novel—this *dernier mot* on robots—was actually begun in 1958, but unfortunately,

> somewhere in the fourth chapter, between one page and the next, something happened. . . .
>
> What that something was is hard to explain. How it is with other writers I can't say, but with me, writing is not actually a conscious and painstaking act of composition and construction. I have within me what the Greeks refer to as a "daimon" and which I refer to as "a little man" that does all the work, and my only part in it is to type very very fast and try to keep up with him.
>
> The only trouble is that he writes what he wants to write, and I can do nothing about it.

Although to date, Asimov has not completed the third novel, the Baley/Daneel team is so popular with science fiction readers that in 1972 he sought to appease them with the short story "Mirror Image." More an exercise in reason and logic than a real story, this attempt has the partners solve the mystery without even leaving Baley's New York City office. Far from appeasing his fans, all Asimov got for his efforts "were a spate of letters saying, 'Thanks, but we mean a *novel*.'"

The novel has not been written. Asimov has, however, provided his readers with a worthy successor, "The Bicentennial Man." Published in 1975, this novella is more fully discussed in Chapter 8.

Each of Asimov's past robot stories and novels added to a growing body of robotic mythology. In the novella "The Bicentennial Man," however, Asimov chose a subject incompatible with the constraints of this lore. And so, exercising the fiction writer's prerogative, he eliminated what he no longer found useful. The result is a parallel world that still admits the inviolate nature of the Three Laws, carries over the names Susan Calvin and U.S. Robots, but discards all other historical precedents.

In past stories, Asimov was concerned with man's reaction to robots. In contrast, "The Bicentennial Man" is the story of one robot's reaction to humanity—Andrew Martin's metamorphosis over the course of two hundred years into a man.

In this version of Earth, man's antipathy to robots has been replaced by wary tolerance; highly specialized robots are widely employed on an Earth possessing a stable robot/human economy and population.

Told from Andrew Martin's viewpoint, this is the first time Asimov has used a robot to narrate its own story, and ironically Andrew Martin is Asimov's most consistently human character. His story is neither a mystery nor a generalized statement on mankind's future; it is the moving account of one being's struggle to realize his potential.

The last of Asimov's robot stories, at least to date, it stands as one of his best. It makes one wish all the more for that third novel.

4

DECLINE AND FALL OF THE EMPIRE: THE FOUNDATION TRILOGY

"The sum of human knowing is beyond any one man; any thousand men. With the destruction of our social fabric, science will be broken into a million pieces. Individuals will know much of exceedingly tiny facets of what there is to know. They will be helpless and useless by themselves. The bits of lore, meaningless will not be passed on. They will be lost through the generations. But, if we now prepare a giant summary of *all* knowledge, it will never be lost."

Foundation

Asimov's most commercially successful work lies in a group of stories and novels known as the "future histories." The Foundation Trilogy, originally an open-ended series of stories published by Campbell in *Astounding Science Fiction*, is Asimov's best known future history. Inspired by Gibbon's *Decline and Fall of the Roman Empire*, Asimov wrote the first stories in the series in an attempt to create "a tale about a far future time written as though it were an historical novel."

When Asimov began to contemplate his future history, Campbell suggested that he follow the example of another *Astounding Science Fiction* writer, Robert Heinlein. Heinlein had meticulously outlined a complete history; this allowed him to write about any period in any order without losing continuity.

Asimov claims to have given this approach a try, but

quickly realized that this was not the way *he* worked. Guided only by the vague direction provided by the course of events in Gibbon's history, he began to write stories that chronologically developed his future history.

As in his other major series, the robot stories, he used a simple device to generate his plots, a development which is only possible if the author is not bound by the requirements of an outline. This method also allowed him, midway through the trilogy, to abandon the Gibbon model and follow the momentum created by the stories themselves.

In the robot stories, the device is the Three Laws; the Foundation Trilogy uses the Seldon Plan: "Hari Seldon was the last great scientist of the First Empire. It was he who brought the science of Psycho-history to its full development." Psycho-history, Asimov tells us, "is the science of human behavior reduced to mathematical equations," a supersociology invented by Asimov for this project. Seldon's equations tell him that this First Galactic Empire is doomed and that it will be followed by 30,000 years of barbarism. Psycho-history, however, provides a partial solution and enables Seldon to devise his plan: by establishing two colonies—the eventual foundations of the Second Empire—at opposite ends of the Galaxy and predetermining their development, he can reduce the 30,000-year-period to a single millennium.

The first book in the trilogy, *Foundation*, opens with Seldon's efforts to establish his colonies in strategic places. Strangely enough, this story is the only segment written out of sequence. When Asimov was collecting his stories for the trilogy, he discovered that his first book, *Foundation*, was too short. Since he had written the stories chronologically, beginning with the first years of the colony called the Foundation, it was impossible to insert any new material. Taking a step backwards, Asimov lifted Hari Seldon out of the Foundation's history books and brought him to life in a new first chapter.

One colony, eventually identified as the Second Foundation, is not mentioned again until midway through the second volume of the trilogy. For the rest of this first book, Asimov deals with the First Foundation as it weathers a series of "Seldon crises."

The Foundation Trilogy is a dramatic history rather than a comprehensive one, and the "Seldon crisis" is an effective method for covering large segments of time. Foreseen by Seldon's equations, each of these crises represents a crucial turning point in the development of the Foundation as it moves towards its psycho-historical destiny. The first book jumps from crisis to crisis as Seldon's First Foundation develops from a single planet of scientists ostensibly preparing a "Galactic Encyclopedia," to the religious center of a small Planetary Federation, to the economic dominance of yet a larger circle of planets, and finally to complete political and economic domination over the entire periphery of the Galaxy.

Most popular histories seem to focus inordinately on the empire-builders' military conquests. Incongruously, Asimov's dramatic future history makes the cogent point that the true tools of empire-building are economic and socio-political development. In large part due to the concept of the Seldon crisis—an inherently dramatic invention—Asimov sacrifices neither drama nor thesis as the chapters of this history unfold.

The first colonists settled on the planet Terminus in the belief that Seldon's Plan would diminish the barbaric interregnum if the most important knowledge of the Galaxy could be gathered in a giant encyclopedia for future generations. They worked on it for fifty years until the first Seldon crisis revealed that the Encyclopedia was an elaborate ruse to conceal Seldon's true plan. With the escalating breakdown of the Empire, the First Foundation found itself cut off from the surviving civilized centers of the Galaxy and threatened by warlike neighbors who have an uncanny resemblance to the Huns.

Seldon's actual plan was to limit the Foundation's alternatives until there was only one solution, the one that would plant the seeds of a Renaissance and a Second Empire. On "an island of atomic power in a growing ocean of more primitive energy," an island that lacked all metals, the Foundationeers could do only one thing—trade their technology for raw materials.

Then follows the era of the Mayors. By surrounding their technology with overtones of fear and superstition—magical sorcery—Terminus is able to export its technical knowledge, receiving in return raw materials, and also exerting a great measure of spiritual influence. Thus they achieve domination, tenuous as it is, over their stronger neighbors.

As this outer region of the Galaxy comes to depend more and more heavily on Terminus for its basic technology, the people of the Foundation realize that the religious trappings are no longer necessary. They now possess a far greater weapon—economic control.

At first this control is extended by the Traders, pioneer-like men who continuously lure new worlds into the Foundation's economic sphere. The concept of trade as a peaceful means of gaining political control was certainly not invented by Asimov. But by giving his Traders certain attributes, attributes closely and easily identified with the American pioneers, he saves them from stereotyped idealism. They are not missionaries advancing the great and glorious cause of the Foundation; they are pragmatic men in a dangerous but monetarily rewarding business, who are mainly concerned wih earning a living. If they help to advance Seldon's plan at the same time, so much the better. If they have any idealism, it springs from their belief in absolute individualism.

The Traders are eventually superseded by the Merchant Princes. Fabulously wealthy, this handful of men controls both Terminus and the entire periphery of the Galaxy. Heredity, not individual initiative, now determines wealth and the power that goes with it. As the initial book of the trilogy ends, the First Foundation has evolved from a small colony of scientists to a federation of plutocrats.

The parallel to Gibbon's history is most discernible in this first book as it depicts the gradual disintegration of a great empire, the concomitant rise in regional trade, and the eventual consolidation of political and economic power in the trading city- (or planet-) states. And like a history, this first book, actually a series of short stories, focuses on mass movements rather than on individual actions.

Foundation and Empire, the second book in the trilogy, is comprised of two novellas, "The General" and "The Mule." With the longer format, Asimov has the freedom to move from this general historical development—a kind of shorthand that enabled him to cover a lot of ground in a relatively short span—to more fully conceived and developed characters.

The book opens two hundred years after Seldon sent his colonists out to the periphery of the Galaxy. Now "the Foundation was the most powerful state in the Galaxy, except for the remains of the Empire, which, concentrated in the central third of the Milky Way, still controlled three-quarters of the population and wealth of the Universe." The time had come for a decisive confrontation between the dying old order and the invincible descendents of Seldon.

In "The General," the forces of the Foundation and the armies of the Empire finally clash. Bel Rios, a general in the Empire's army, is so popular and so successful that the Emperor and the court feel threatened by him. Rios is banished to the ends of the Universe. His ambition undaunted, he seeks new conquests and stumbles across the rich worlds of the Foundation.

For its part, the Foundation has entered a socially rigid period. With the wealth and power held by the Merchant Princes, the Foundation is divided into "haves and have nots." When the brilliant Rios initiates his campaign by attacking the Outer Worlds of the Foundation's federation, they fall quickly. The Foundation's leaders find themselves unable to defeat Rios.

Obviously this is another Seldon crisis, a crisis which they expect to overcome despite all evidence to the contrary. Nevertheless, they find themselves defeated in every major battle; the rigid and conservative Merchant Princes are no match for the vigorous and imaginative Rios as he moves his armies closer and closer to Terminus, home of the Foundation.

But Seldon's vision holds true, and the Foundation's victory is inevitable. Inexplicably, Rios is recalled by the Emperor and executed as a traitor. Rios' defeat is a "psycho-historical necessity." As one character explains it, the social climate of the Empire makes successful wars of conquest impossible. The Emperor is willing to tolerate anything but strong subjects. If they are weak, they pose no threat to his throne. If they are strong, like Bel Rios, they can be banished to the frontier. However, if they persist in winning popular victories, they must be eliminated.

It would seem that Asimov had painted himself into a corner—the Plan appears to be foolproof. Asimov would be forced to continue repeating the same formula—a Seldon crisis followed by a period of upheaval that ends with a sudden revelation of a Seldon solution—as long as *Astounding Science Fiction*'s readers continued to demand Foundation stories.

Fortunately Campbell suggested strongly, over Asimov's protests, that the Seldon Plan be upset. The result was "The Mule."

One of Seldon's basic assumptions in predicting human behavior is "that human reactions to stimuli would remain constant." Dealing with human behavior on a galactic scale, a scale which statistically negates the exceptional individual, Seldon had not considered the possibility of a single positive mutation, one individual who could make Seldon's statistical predictions meaningless by altering human reactions.

In the second part of *Foundation and Empire* an obscure warlord known only as the Mule is creating panic in the Galaxy, quickly conquering world after world and drawing them into his new Empire. At first the Foundationeers see him as yet another in a long line of petty warlords, conquerors who come and go with regularity now that the Empire has completely crumbled. Even when he attacks the Foundation, they view it as a minor irritation, convinced that Seldon's plan is invincible. Only when the Foundation has completely fallen, do they realize that the Mule is a mutant with peculiar powers, a variable unforeseen by Seldon.

When things look darkest, Seldon's disciples recall his vague references to a Second Foundation. Desperate to save the Plan and avoid the projected thirty thousand years of barbarism, a small group of refugee Foundationeers begins to search for the elusive Second Foundation.

The search takes on greater urgency when the refugees discover that the Mule, too, is on the trail of the Second Foundation. Asimov has created a formidable foe in the Mule, one particularly suited to upset the psycho-historical plan that rests on the basic assumption that human reactions will remain constant. Only after the first Foundation has been destroyed does the extent of his power become apparent—his mutation allows him to control and manipulate human emotions. As the Mule describes it, "To me, men's minds are dials, with pointers that indicate the prevailing emotion . . . I learned that I could reach into those minds and turn the pointer to the spot I wished, that I could nail it there forever."

A less imaginative writer might have presented the struggle between the powerful Mule and the remnants of the Foundations as a confrontation between good and evil.

Asimov always avoids the obvious—things are rarely what they seem. But here this technique is especially effective. In the first pages of the story, the refugees—Trader Torin, his wife Batya, and the Foundation scientist, Mis Ebling— have picked up Magnifico, the runaway jester of the Mule. He is as scrawny and craven as his name is grand. Torin and Batya take pity on him; Batya, especially, feels protective toward the runaway, and he becomes a member of the party as they seem to stay one step ahead of the Mule.

But the Mule is closer than they suspect. As the story reaches its climax, it becomes clear to Batya that all along they have been doing the Mule's bidding, manipulated by him as surely and effectively as those he has conquered. The sad, gentle jester, she realizes, is the Mule.

The technique of integrating the Mule into the story as a sympathetic character allows Asimov to explore the more human aspects of political upheaval and armed conquest.

Although the Mule is the enemy of the Seldon Plan, his aims are no less noble than Seldon's. He wants to reunite the fragments of the old civilization into a second Empire. (Without the vision that psycho-history provides, he cannot realize that his empire will die with him.) His victories are as bloodless as any of the Foundation's economic and religious manipulations. He infiltrates each world, adjusting the emotions of its inhabitants so that they lay down their arms and surrender. He repays Batya's kindness to the ugly misshapen jester by refusing to tamper with her emotions and by sparing her and her husband even though at the last minute, she snatches victory from his grasp.

Batya is a character well worth a closer look. Asimov calls her his "first successful, well-rounded female character." When the story opens, the reader assumes that Torin, Batya's husband, is the protagonist; but as it progresses, we see that it is Batya who possesses the archetypal characteristics of the hero—stamina, intelligence, initiative, courage, and compassion. Despite Asimov's belief, his marriage of woman and hero is not without flaws. His basic feminine stereotypes creep in: Batya is given motherly instincts, is shown cooking meals for all the men, and tidying up the spaceship while her husband attends to the important business of flying the ship. Apparently Asimov was unable to conceive of a female character without these qualities until almost thirty years later in *The Gods Themselves.*

In the stories that comprise the first half of the trilogy, there is almost a mechanical quality as people follow Seldon's blueprint. When Campbell asked Asimov to upset the Seldon Plan, it forced Asimov to move away from the Gibbon parallel. What Campbell may not have foreseen was that Asimov would also replace his broad historical development with more intricate stories revolving around more subtle characterization.

The first three hundred pages of the Foundation's history are interesting, but when the Mule makes his appearance, he seems to leap out of the pages. Now Asimov's intellectual involvement has a complementary emotional component. Characters no longer simply illustrate the galactic upheaval—they *live* through it. The trilogy hits its peak with the creation of the Mule. Showman that he is, Asimov does not abandon him at the end of *Foundation and Empire.* Instead, he implies that the Mule's reign is far from over.

The final book, the *Second Foundation,* opens with the Mule's continued search for that mysterious hidden colony. Like everyone else, the Mule assumes that the Second Foundation has concentrated on the development of Seldon's mathematical psychology much in the way that the First Foundation concentrated on technological development. Now that the First Foundation has proved no match for the Mule, and the old empire has completely disintegrated, only the mastery of the human psyche by the Second stands between him and total domination of the Galaxy.

In the two novellas—"Search by the Mule" and "Search by the Foundation"—that make up this final volume, Asimov divides his characters into two classifications: those tampered with and those who act with free will. Han Pritcher, a minor character in the previous Mule story, typifies the psychologically controlled in "Search by the Mule." A general in the Mule's army, Pritcher has been unsuccessfully searching for the Second Foundation. In the opening chapter, he is forced to hand over command of his expedition to Bal Channis, a man with whose mind the Mule has chosen not to tamper.

As the Mule explains to the converted Pritcher, "When you lost your native motivations, you lost something, some subtle drive, that I cannot possibly replace." He hopes that the unconverted Channis, motivated by ambition and not by instilled loyalty, will succeed where Pritcher failed.

When the story gets underway, however, we see that Asimov's classification is a charade; there are only those tampered with and those tampered with more subtly. Channis has been skillfully altered by the Second Foundation in order to lead the Mule into a trap. By the end of the story, even the Mule's powerful mind proves vulnerable to manipulation. Seldon's descendents are able to erase totally from his mind the notion of a Second Foundation. No longer driven by ambition, the Mule becomes a man of peace and lives out his years as a contented ruler of his kingdom.

This type of plot where nothing is what it seems and where each character is manipulated by the author's desire to keep the reader constantly off balance is an irritating aspect of Asimov's work. It's almost as if the reader has been presented with one of those mathematical brain teasers, an artificial structure that has no place in this type of fiction. This characteristic is annoying in "Search by the Mule"; it is even more distracting in the second half of the book, "Search by the Foundation."

Asimov had wanted to end the Foundation series with "Search by the Mule," but Campbell insisted that he do one more story. Asimov agreed but only if he could reveal the location of the Second Foundation and provide a logical conclusion to the series. Campbell accepted the compromise but only after extracting a promise from Asimov that it be fifty thousand words.

Since Asimov had been so pleased with his creation, Batya, in *Foundation and Empire*, he resurrects her in the form of her fourteen-year-old granddaughter, Arcadia, the heroine of "Search by the Foundation." As in the rest of the Foundation series, this book focuses on political intrigue rather than on battles. Any battles are referred to only in passing, and unfortunately, as in "Search by the Mule," all action results from vague psychological tampering. This time it is the Second Foundation which is responsible for the manipulation of people's minds, and no one is immune, not even Arcadia, who has been controlled since birth.

"Search by the Foundation" was not written with the facility that is so characteristic of Asimov's writing. As he says in his autobiography, "I disliked it intensely and found working on it very difficult." One problem was that "each Foundation story assumes, as a background, all the previous stories." And since they were published as a serial, it was his job to incorporate that information into each story. As the series grew longer and longer, it became increasingly difficult to do this without obvious contrivance. By the time he reaches, "Search by the Foundation," Asimov resorts to a history class term paper prepared by young Arcadia.

Although this recapitulation made it tiresome for Asimov, it's possible for readers to skip over it. What the readers cannot escape is the erratic plot that twists and turns rather than develops. They are also forced to endure characters who rarely move beyond the stereotype: Homer Munn, the timid librarian; Lady Callia, the dumb, beautiful mistress who is really the power behind the throne; Preem Palver, the old Jewish merchant who is kind and wise as well as soft-hearted. (Perhaps one indication of Asimov's weariness with the series is Palver's speech. Here in the far, far distant future is a man who speaks in the cadences of New York's lower East Side.)

While Arcadia is not a stereotype, she possesses so many heroic attributes that she is far less human than her grandmother, Batya. Given the plot premise, there was little room for a more human character; if Arcadia were less than perfect, there would be no story at all.

As a serial in *Astounding Science Fiction*, the Foundation Trilogy was popular with readers; in book format, it has become a classic. It is arguably Asimov's best-known work of science fiction and certainly the most widely read. His peers acknowledged its special quality when in 1966 the trilogy earned a special Hugo Award for the best all-time science fiction series. If there are so many imperfections in the Foundation Trilogy, how does one account for its success and its claim on most readers' imaginations?

On the simplest level, the series' structure is inherently appealing. Each story builds on its predecessors, involving readers more and more deeply. In a certain sense, the reader becomes a vicarious participant in Asimov's developing history, a history which has the additional fascination of a conclusion.

Asimov's style in the Foundation, as in most of his work, has a positive quality that is frequently overlooked. Commendably direct, his writing never gets in the way of the story, yet rarely seems unequal to its task. He always opens with a moment of crisis, and even if his characters indulge in long explanations, there is always the illusion of action.

Despite the overall length of the series, the reader easily moves from story to story.

In large part, science fiction readers have been intrigued by the novelty of Asimov's all-human Galaxy. Without aliens—often distracting science fiction gimmicks—he must provide recognizable human motives for galactic enterprises. An alien Mule might have provided novelty. A human Mule has the depth to dominate his third of the trilogy.

But the most fascinating element is the depiction of a human society's development. The members of the society are so easily recognizable that the trilogy strikes the reader as an actual history. It seems like a simple recitation of events that have already occurred instead of speculation about a future time. We read history to discover why things happen. The "what if" premise underlying most science fiction places a certain intellectual distance between the reader and the story. Asimov has managed to eliminate this distance with his concept of future history. The reader does not actually believe that these events did occur; the important thing is that he/she never questions that they could.

When we follow any history over hundreds of years, we can perceive in an individual's actions the resultant far-reaching social effects. Seldon's seemingly insignificant act—the establishment of a small colony—snowballs until it is ultimately responsible for guiding human destiny for the next millennia.

In the Foundation Trilogy, Asimov provides his readers with the pleasure of watching this type of ripple effect. As a result, the scope of Asimov's history fascinates in a way that is analogous to the appeal of *The Decline and Fall of the Roman Empire*. The successful transfer of this historical perspective to science fiction is, more than any other single element, one of Asimov's greatest fictional inventions.

5

GALACTIC STRUGGLE: THE FUTURE HISTORIES

"To the rest of the Galaxy, if they are aware of us at all, Earth is but a pebble in the sky."

Pebble in the Sky

Incidental to the historical sequence of the Foundation Trilogy but using the same general time frame, are the four future history novels: *Pebble in the Sky, The Currents of Space, The Stars, Like Dust,* and *The End of Eternity.* Unlike the Foundation stories, these books were written as novels and later serialized in the pulp magazines.

Pebble in the Sky, Asimov's very first novel, is set in the early years of a Galactic Empire. The tens of thousands of inhabited planets in the Galaxy have been united under the rule of the planet Trantor, although each has retained its cultural autonomy. The action takes place on Earth, a poor, despised radioactive planet whose position as the birthplace of humanity has been lost to history.

As a result of a nuclear mishap, Joseph Schwartz, a retired tailor living in the Chicago of 1949, is in an instant transported into this far distant future. Confused, unsure of his own sanity—nothing corresponds with his memory of the world, not the language, the society, not even the landscape—he is unwittingly drawn into a plot by Earth's ruling zealots to avenge centuries of discrimination by releasing a science fiction version of the bubonic plague on the rest of the Galaxy.

The theme of prejudice in its various manifestations is often to be found in Asimov's work. *Pebble in the Sky* deals with the personal indignities that colonialism fosters, even a colonialism that emanates from the most democratic government, be it national or galactic. To the rest of the Galaxy, the people of Earth seem barbarous, superstitious, repulsive carriers of radioactivity, and as such, are shunned and their serious economic problems ignored. The "Earthie," as he is contemptuously termed, lives a life of austere poverty in a society which practices euthanasia—ridding itself of all unproductive members and anyone reaching the age of sixty—and which imposes the death sentence for even minor infractions of religious taboos. Disciplined with an iron fist by disdainful soldiers of the Empire, the people of Earth are even denied permission to emigrate to the more prosperous planets of the Galaxy.

Schwartz is an unusual hero for science fiction. He is sixty-two, a European immigrant who would have been content to enjoy the comforts of old age. Stubborn, not in the least idealistic, wanting desperately to return to his own world—a world that is gone—Schwartz wants only to die, and he even rejects the opportunity to thwart the zealots' revenge. It is not his Galaxy, and he does not care if it "rots and dies."

What makes Schwartz most unusual is that he is not "heroic." Most of his actions seem motivated by crankiness and a feisty independence rather than an idealized sense of justice and right. His reactions are realistic—when he finds himself in an alien landscape, he does not brilliantly deduce that he has been transported to the future, but rather, he thinks as any of us would, "I'm insane!"

As a prisoner he does not concoct an intricate or dramatic plan of escape; he simply walks out of a door that has accidentally been left open. Even at the very end, arguments that rely on an abstract sense of justice fail to move him; only when he perceives a relationship between the galactic crisis and his own life as an immigrant, does he decide to join the forces of good.

In writing about far-distant times, science fiction writers, Asimov included, often manipulate their characters like chess pieces in a master game plan. Although Schwartz is offstage for at least half the book, he anchors the story in a world of realistic motives and actions, a world of flesh-and-blood people. The aura of humanness that surrounds Schwartz casts its glow on the other characters. Lord Ennius, the Empire's representative on Earth, is more than just a symbol of colonialism. Homesick for his own lush planet, he gauges all of his administrative decisions by their potential effects on his career as a diplomat. He resents the fact that he is buried in one of the Empire's backwater planets, but makes a conscientious effort to carry out his duties as well as he can.

Even a minor character, like the crippled farmer whose family is hiding him from the authorities, is rich in the ambiguity of human motives. He feels guilty about endangering his family, but he's afraid to die in the prescribed program of euthanasia. This is no lovable old man—his demands make life difficult for his family—yet his affection for them is clear.

The overall impression conveyed by the characters in *Pebble in the Sky*, despite the galactic scale of this future history, is that each individual is important. In a world where the expendability of life is a premise that the society accepts, the members of the crippled farmer's family, of their own volition, risk their lives to keep him alive. Schwartz's final decision reflects this same emphasis on individual will. The totalitarian society of the future runs the same risks that those of the past have faced. There will always, Asimov implies, be individuals who rebel, who isolate themselves from the mass to determine their own paths.

Asimov is not above a simplistic representation of prejudice: helpless women are reviled by soldiers because they are Earthwomen—and "inferior." No space traveler would consider touching one. But *Pebble in the Sky* goes far beyond this type of naive illustration. Prejudice is shown as the diminution of individuals, not only the direct objects of it such as Schwartz and the farmer, but also Lord Ennius, who in enforcing racism is subtly crippled by it.

This depiction is possible because Asimov has avoided the pitfall of creating symbolic characters to illustrate a moral. Instead he emphasizes each character's human qualities, his or her quirks, strengths and weaknesses, and is successful in exploring a theme that is too often sentimentalized in popular fiction.

The Currents of Space, published in 1952, interweaves political intrigue and racism. In contrast to *Pebble in the Sky*, this book has no real hero, although it abounds in heroic idealism. Set at a time when Trantor is on the verge of establishing the Galactic Empire, the story deals with the exploitation of an agricultural planet by a neighboring planet and its ruling aristocrats. Like the pre-Civil War South, Florina has one crop—in this case, kyrt, a fiber highly prized throughout the Galaxy for its combination of beauty and strength. Literally worth its weight in gold, it can only grow on Florina and is the source of the ruling planet Sark's immense wealth and power.

On Florina the life of the population is one of virtual slavery. There are native overseers—the Townsmen—who are part of the civil service and who are responsible for the smooth running of the government machinery.

One main character, a Townsman, has been plotting for years to overthrow his oppressors, the ruling Squires of Sark. As his plot gains momentum, his idealism drives him to measures that are more fanatical than idealistic. After years of careful planning, the Townsman's values show the first signs of corruption when he maims an innocent man simply to ensure his silence. From this point, it is easy to justify exposing his fellow Florinians to possible annihilation and finally to justify random, cold-blooded murder.

Other protagonists are also motivated by variations of this type of twisted idealism. The ambassador who represents Trantor, the most powerful political force in the Galaxy, is dedicated to galactic peace, a goal achievable, he believes, in the near future. Paradoxically, he is willing to sacrifice the entire Florinian population if it is the only way to keep that peace. For the book's representative scientist, all political systems must bow to a pangalactic search for scientific truth. Each in his own way holds a set of ideals that justifies any action, no matter how repugnant or immoral.

On the other hand there is Valona, the book's major female character. Although she espouses no lofty ideals, her actions truly embody loyalty, love, self-sacrifice—her values are evident in her actions.

In *Pebble in the Sky* the complex characterization of Schwartz continues throughout the book. However, in *The Currents of Space*, one apt adjective could have been used to sum up the essence of each character and justify his or her actions. The book is further flawed by its more naive treatment of racism; the complex problem is reduced to stereotyped interaction between victim and oppressor.

The third book, *The Stars, Like Dust*, combines science fiction with many elements of another popular pulp genre—the western. In a world of good guys and bad guys, Biron Farrill, "six feet, two inches of hard musculature," goes forth to avenge the execution of his father, the Rancher of Widemos. Like the typical cowboy hero, Biron epitomizes courage, valor, physical strength, fair play, and is pitted against his father's betrayer, a "rat," who seeks personal gain under the guise of idealism.

Just as typically, both hero and villain pursue the same woman, Artemisia, "a smoldering girl, dark of hair and eyes." When armed, Biron carries a futuristic version of the six-gun, a neuronic whip, in each hand; when his adversary is disarmed, Biron is always willing to fight "man to man."

The plot is as convoluted as the characterization is simple. A story of empire builders and rebel worlds, it is rife with agents, counter-agents, and counter-counter-agents. Like the giver of the prankster's gift that is simply a box within a box within a box, Asimov reveals a series of motives for each character's actions, each one more complex than the last. The net effect is that the reader suffers a dizziness akin to the space vertigo that Asimov has invented for this novel.

Asimov does, however, posit certain intriguing ideas incidental to the plot, which if developed, might have resulted in a more substantial, although perhaps more cynical book. As one character sees it, the only science man has ever explored totally has been the science of war. Shifting perspectives reveal that even a freedom-fighter can represent oppression to those under his control, and only when people become rebels are they able to perceive the signs of social and moral decay all around them.

Strictly speaking, *The End of Eternity* is not a future history, but its setting is closest to the populated Galaxy of the Foundation Trilogy. In a way this is an alternative picture of the Foundation Galaxy, a parallel reality that emphasizes time travel rather than space travel. By the end of the story we learn that if allowed to continue its existence, this parallel reality would prevent the formation of a Galactic Empire.

In this story, Eternity has a special meaning. It is a bureaucracy whose agents move forward and backward in time to effect changes which they have determined will lead to the most desirable reality. For the members of Eternity, a select group, reality is always a question of choice; any given reality is only one of a number of possible alternatives.

Though as a scientist, Asimov considers time travel an impossibility, *The End of Eternity* is his attempt to deal with every paradox of time travel and is built around a love story between an Eternal—a man out of time—and a woman firmly rooted in time, an agent from the only reality that has chosen to eliminate Eternity. Since paradoxes are by definition contradictory, Asimov begs the question by burying the paradoxes of time travel in a complex plot, a plot that gives the reader little time or opportunity to question the illogicality of the book's central premise, the possibility of time travel. For example, the inventor of time travel is sent from the future to the century of his discovery by means of his own invention. Like a magician, Asimov misdirects the reader's attention by adroitly introducing a dramatic race to prevent the collapse of Eternity. Having avoided the plausibility of its existence throughout eighteen chapters, Asimov ends the book by simply allowing Eternity to vanish in a puff of smoke.

Once again, nothing is what it seems, and the plot resembles an extended puzzle designed to act as a smoke screen to cover flaws.

The convoluted plotting so visible in *The End of Eternity* and *The Stars, Like Dust* is perhaps the worst trait evident in much of Asimov's work. And yet, paradoxically, it seems directly related to the process that has resulted in some of his best work. Asimov seems to generate his plots by starting with a given premise and attempting to discover the least obvious implication of it. The process appears to be a deliberate, cognitive one, much like that of a laboratory scientist testing proofs of hypotheses by trial-and-error experimentation.

This process has led to successful works such as "Nightfall," the majority of the robot stories, *The Caves of Steel*, *The Naked Sun*, and later "The Bicentennial Man" and *The Gods Themselves*. In each of these, although it is evident that this cognitive process provides a starting point, the story itself quickly takes over with a momentum of its own. "Nightfall," for example, had its genesis in a quotation: "If the stars should appear one night in a thousand years, how would men believe and adore, and preserve for many generations the remembrance of the city of God?" It seems logical that a writer methodically exploring the implications of this quote might hit on the idea that men would react to their first sight of stars with superstitious hysteria. But at some point in the writing, Asimov took the creative leap that makes this story endure as one of his best—he suggests that the real terror of this event would be the awesome revelation of a single world's insignificance in a universe crowded with millions of worlds.

Often, however, a story or novel fails to move beyond its initial stage. *The End of Eternity* and *The Stars, Like Dust* are not the only examples of this failing. It mars both "Search by the Mule" and "Search by the Foundation" in *Second Foundation*, "The Black Friar of the Flame," and some of the robot stories including "Risk" and "The Life and Times of Multivac." In each case the story never takes over as Asimov substitutes plot manipulation for plot development. The reader constantly senses the presence of the author rather than of the character. While this may cause no problems in Agatha Christie's mysteries, it has a disastrous effect in science fiction. The science fiction reader, expecting to be transported to a possible future, wants the illusion of this future to be a seamless one.

Asimov is certainly capable of sustaining illusion as he has shown over and over from his first novel, *Pebble in the Sky* to his most recent, *The Gods Themselves*. How then can one account for the plots which resemble puzzles, rather than plots that act as frameworks for fully developed fiction, plots that continually puncture illusion as they twist and turn? Perhaps an answer is suggested by looking at the two Mule novellas which make up a substantial part of the Foundation Trilogy.

The Mule appears for the first time in a story that is easily the high point of the Foundation Trilogy. Called simply, "The Mule," this story is dominated by its central character, a character never subordinated to the machinations of plot. This is a story about him rather than a story about events in which he happens to play a part. Asimov creates the illusion of a fascinating historical figure so skillfully that even the subordinate characters share in this fictional reality.

When the character reappears in "Search by the Mule," he has been reduced to a game piece. His actions no longer stem from character. Instead Asimov has substituted an intricate plot that relies on constant revelations intended to startle the reader. Here the function of the Mule and all the other characters is to act as agents of the plot. The result is an inferior sequel.

It would be convenient to attribute the first story to inspiration and the second to imitation of a successful formula. Unfortunately the facts do not support this theory. "The Mule" was written on orders from *Astounding Science Fiction* editor, John Campbell. Conversely Asimov wrote "Search by the Mule," originally called "Now You See It . . .," without any prodding by Campbell.

Asimov began to fulfill Campbell's request to upset the Seldon Plan "rather sulkily." But apparently once he got caught up in the story, his initial lack of enthusiasm was forgotten, and he found himself working "rapidly, more rapidly than I had at any other time during the war [World War II]." It is evident that at some point the creative artist took over and when the dust cleared, Asimov found: "It was the very first story I had ever written that was so long, that had so intricate a plot, and that had so lengthy a cast of characters."

"Search by the Mule" was, Asimov says, to be the final Foundation story. ". . . I had grown a little weary of the Foundation and all its works. I had been working on it, on and off, for five years. I had written seven stories, totalling about 185,000 words. I felt it was time to end the thing and get on to something new."

This desire to be finished with the Foundation Trilogy may account in part for the lackluster quality of the story. But another factor must be considered, a factor that has some bearing on all of Asimov's early work. A large portion of his income depended on science fiction. Had he possessed the luxury of writing more leisurely, he might have found it possible to write with a more critical eye and to discard a foundering story. But as his autobiography points out, he was determined to make his living as a writer and placed great importance on the money his stories brought him. "Search by the Mule" earned him $500 when it was published in *Astounding Science Fiction*. It seems reasonable to assume that when the other stories and novels are more intellectual exercise than fiction, they are the work of a writer falling back on secondary resources when inspiration flags.

While *Currents of Space, The Stars, Like Dust,* and *The End of Eternity* seem in varying degrees to fit this assumption, they are saved by the depths of their author's imagination. They lack interesting characterization and rely on stereotype stock characters. More critically, they lack the historical sweep of the Foundation Trilogy. Yet they are sprinkled with intriguing concepts and ideas that, though often presented as asides that have little to do with the plot, continue to reward the reader's interest.

In *Currents of Space* Asimov begins to probe the force of idealism; as it moves into the realm of fanatacism, he equates its methods and effects with political opportunism. The only character who exhibits a superior moral quality is the one who never feels the need to explain or justify her actions; her actions, not her words, illustrate her morality. Asimov seems to connect the desire for power over others, wielded by idealist and opportunist alike, to a facility for self-deception. The only person capable of ethical motives is the one incapable of such self-deception. These are thought-provoking observations, but the novel is incapable of exploiting them to their best advantage. As a tale of adventure and mystery, the vehicle is not equal to the concepts.

Idealism is again portrayed as a justification for any expedient action, even murder, in *The Stars, Like Dust*. It is evident that Asimov is intrigued by the relationship of individual and state, and while they are not integrated successfully into the plot, his thoughts on that relationship are the imaginative high points of the novel. The perception of oppression and moral decay is shown to depend on the character's vantage point; those loyal to a political system may see a government's use of force as justified, while those in opposition will see the same act as one of tyranny.

The End of Eternity shows that even a benign form of idealism can be pernicious. Without violence the government in this novel attempts to iron out all the difficulties facing the human race. Once again Asimov places the state in opposition to individual freedom. In the pursuit of its goals this government executes no one; instead, it identifies individuals whose acts will have "undesirable" effects on the future and simply alters reality so that they will never have existed.

This novel yields more than a few worthwhile asides, and it rests on an imaginative premise. The bulk of science fiction deals with humanity's exploration of space. In *The End of Eternity* Asimov suggests that humanity may ignore space travel as it expends its considerable energies exploring that fourth dimension, time.

The difficulty here is that Asimov gets so involved in the various implications of time travel that he comes to treat the plot primarily as a device for illustrating them. The breakdown in the story line is so complete that by the novel's end the hero's questions seem designed to provide an opportunity for the heroine to clarify troublesome aspects of the plot.

In contrast, Asimov never bothers to explain clearly how Joseph Schwartz was transported from 1949 to an unspecified time in the far distant future. The plot in *Pebble in the Sky* lacks the complexity of the later novel and uses far simpler motivations for actions. Why then is *Pebble in the Sky* the better book?

The answer lies in the characters. This novel combines a humanistic appreciation of the individual with a speculative yet realistic depiction of a future world. And while even the minor characters in this novel impress the reader as individuals, Joseph Schwartz, the embodiment of this humanistic appreciation, is distinctive among science fiction characters. Other writers have transported contemporary men to the future, but only Asimov would have the audacity to choose a retired immigrant from Chicago. More to the point, Asimov is not seduced by the novelty of the situation. Instead, he has created a story about the development of this character in a completely imaginative world, a development that is a prime requirement of mainstream fiction but often of secondary importance in genre works.

For this reason, *Pebble in the Sky* must be ranked among Asimov's best.

6

SPACE OPERA: THE LUCKY STARR BOOKS

"You should have a name which would indicate your travels through space; the way in which you range from one end of the universe to the other. If I were a creature such as yourself, it seems to me that it would be fitting I should be called 'Space Ranger'."

David Starr, Space Ranger

Considering all the attention normally received by Asimov's work, it is surprising to note that he has written another series, roughly equivalent to the Foundation Trilogy, which in critical reviews is mentioned only in passing, if at all. Asimov's name is always linked with the Foundation and his robots, but even his fans are not always aware of his "juvenile" novels, the six Lucky Starr books.

The series was conceived early in 1952 when his editor at Doubleday, Walter Bradbury, suggested that Asimov create a hero that could be adapted to a television series and earn them both "an honest dollar." Asimov's only objection was that the television producers might "ruin my stories and I would be ashamed to be identified with them." Bradbury suggested a pseudonym and Asimov agreed. Whimsically influenced by Cornell Woolrich, whose nom de plume was William Irish, Asimov crossed the channel and took the name of Paul French.

With a television audience in mind from the inception, an audience which seemed to love horse operas like "The Lone Ranger" and "The Cisco Kid," he created a space opera whose hero was a Space Ranger.

David Starr, called Lucky by all who know him, is everything a space opera hero should be: he is tall, good-looking, thin but muscular, intelligent, athletic, has a well-developed sense of right and wrong, and is the man to call upon when the situation seems hopeless. The fact that Lucky was orphaned when his parents were killed by space pirates is also well-calculated. There is no concerned family to encumber his wanderings through space, and he has a justifiable motive for his struggles against evil.

All television heroes require a sidekick. The Lone Ranger has Tonto; the Cisco Kid has Pancho, and Lucky Starr has John Bigman Jones. Since sidekicks must complement rather than compete with the hero, Bigman is short (5′1″), hot-tempered, pugnacious, and of course, unquestionably loyal, as well as a good man to have around in a fight.

Five of the books take place on different planets in our solar system—Mercury, Venus, Mars, Saturn, and Jupiter. The sixth takes place in the asteroid belt between Jupiter and Mars. A seventh, planned but never written, would have taken Lucky to Pluto.

Although he relies on a stock plot—the hero saving our solar system from its enemies in the Galaxy—Asimov typically puts his individual stamp on the stories; the physical setting of each story is, given the knowledge of the time, accurate. Unfortunately Asimov had the bad luck to be writing these stories on the threshold of an unprecedented exploration of our solar system's planets, an exploration which has immensely increased our astronomical knowledge. Many of his scientific premises, sound in 1952, were later found to be inaccurate. In an attempt to avoid misleading the reader into accepting outdated conjecture as fact, Asimov has added prefaces to the new Fawcett editions of the Lucky Starr books, published in 1971.

David Starr, Space Ranger, the first book in the series, takes place on Mars, whose farms supply the greater part of Earth's agricultural products.

When a plot which would cut Earth off from its essential food supply is uncovered, David Starr is sent to Mars on his first assignment as a member of the Council of Science, a semisecret, all-powerful organization charged with interplanetary law enforcement, a kind of galactic FBI.

Working undercover as a farmhand, David meets and befriends John Bigman Jones, a small tough "farm boy," born and bred on Mars. The two escape numerous attempts on their lives, and as might be expected, bring the culprits to justice.

In the course of events, Asimov orchestrates David's rites of passage from young man to "Space Ranger." Exploring the planet's caverns, David discovers native Martian intelligences—beings that have evolved beyond a physical state into a state of pure energy. These beings sense David's basic goodness and, dubbing him "Space Ranger," charge him with the mission to fight the criminal and warlike tendencies of the human race so that ultimately humans may prove to be "a companion in eternity" to the Martian race. To aid David in this mission, they provide him with an unearthly energy shield which protects him and disguises his identity.

This scene is the high point of the book and one that briefly takes it out of the realm of space opera. And, in a way, it foreshadows what Asimov would do so splendidly over twenty years later in *The Gods Themselves*.

Feeling that the name, David, was too "pedestrian," Asimov changed it to Lucky in his second book, *Lucky Starr and the Pirates of the Asteroids*. Published in 1953, this is the only one in the series that remains scientifically accurate. "If I had to write the novel today," Asimov says, "I would hardly have to change a word."

The Asteroid Belt has become a haven for all the lawless elements in our solar system; worse, still, these pirates may now be the allies of Earth's bitterest foes, humans from the Sirian system. On a more personal level, these are the pirates who murdered Lucky's parents. In true space opera fashion, Lucky Starr not only cleans out the nest of pirates and avenges his parents' deaths, but succeeds in averting war with the Sirians.

During his battle with the pirates, Lucky has occasion to use his Martian shield. Perhaps Asimov was growing weary of overloading his series with stereotypical elements, because this is the last time the shield is mentioned; also, the title "Space Ranger" is never alluded to again.

The most interesting element of *Lucky Starr and the Oceans of Venus* is another of Asimov's alien creations— the V-Frogs. V-Frogs are cute little aquatic oddities that inspire affection through a crude type of emotional control over those who come in contact with them. Since all of Venus is covered by a single ocean, these frogs are quite common and almost everyone living in the planet's domed cities has one as a pet. When a mad genius invents a machine that allows him to control huge numbers of these frogs, and through them, human beings, the colony on Venus is threatened. Lucky discovers the method by which the V-Frogs are being used to manipulate people and puts an end to the mad scientist's dictatorial ambitions.

Although the plot does not withstand critical scrutiny, and even though we now know that there is no ocean on Venus, Asimov's description of aquatic animal and plant forms, as well as human life in underwater cities, is so graphic that the book is often engrossing.

The weakest of the six books is *Lucky Starr and the Big Sun of Mercury*. Here the mechanics of the plot are visible to the most superficial reader. Puppet-like characters react predictably, and by now the limitations of the Bigman character—his stock response to insulting references to his size, his mother-like concern for Lucky's safety—have become grating. The only thing of interest in this book is the introduction of robots and the Three Laws of Robotics to the series. While he continued to write as Paul French, his mention of the Three Laws was as good as a personal signature.

Written in 1957 and 1958 respectively, *Lucky Starr and the Moons of Jupiter* and *Lucky Starr and the Rings of Saturn* both reflect the political insecurities engendered by the Cold War. Sirius bears more than a superficial resemblance to the then-current American view of Russia as it constantly maneuvers to gain both scientific and military advantage over Earth. The weapons here are spies and sabre-rattling, operating in an atmosphere of thinly veiled hostility.

In *The Moons of Jupiter,* Sirian spies have infiltrated one of Earth's most important research projects—the development of an anti-gravity propulsion system. Situated on one of Jupiter's outer moons, the project has been the subject of repeated security checks. Yet no leaks have been uncovered, and the Sirians continue to receive up-to-date information on all areas of the project, areas that no single man has access to. As the first prototype of the system is being prepared for testing, Lucky is sent to the site in a last-ditch effort to destroy the spy ring.

Lucky soon realizes that the spy must be a robot and attempts to discover which of the suspects is governed by the Three Laws. Only at the very end does he realize that he has been tricked by his own preconceptions; like most readers of Asimov's robot fiction, Lucky has expected the robot to be humanoid. When the evidence becomes so overwhelming that the possibility can no longer be overlooked, he identifies a blind man's Seeing-Eye dog as the robot.

Characteristically Asimovian is the utilization of the unexpected in a plot twist. In this case, Asimov takes advantage of the fact that the word robot connotes mechanical man. It is true that any perceptive reader immediately becomes suspicious when he introduces for the first time in any of his books a handicapped character who is in on all the action. If this is not enough, the blind engineer has a Seeing-Eye dog, an obvious anachronism in such a highly technical environment.

Yet Asimov's description of the anti-gravity system, whether it is used to propel an elevator or a ship, is so plausible and so graphically explained that it draws the reader into the story. We begin to react to the characters as people, and Asimov's moons of Jupiter take on an enjoyable appearance of reality. The book easily overcomes the weak mystery element.

The situation in the last and best book of the series, *Lucky Starr and the Rings of Saturn,* is one in which Earth is threatened by Sirian encroachment on our solar system—Sirius has set up a military base on Titan, Saturn's largest moon. As the birthplace of humanity, Earth is resented by the other worlds of the Galaxy, all former colonies. Earth's leaders know that if they declare war on the Sirians, the majority of the other worlds will side with the enemy. In an attempt to avoid such a war, Earth calls an intergalactic conference. Here in the book's dramatic high point, Lucky, against all odds, engineers a coup. The unallied worlds censure Sirius and order them to abandon Titan.

This novel goes a great deal beyond space opera. It goes far beyond simple action to deal with social, ethical, and political motives. For the first time in the series we see the enemy face to face, and he is no less intelligent nor less honorable than we are. Our strengths lie in what other societies have labeled weaknesses: suspicion of the overuse of technology; the belief that individuality and variety are positive traits; and that the goals of genetic superiority and social conformity are destructive ones.

The label "juvenile" does not seem to fit this novel, nor, in fact, any of the series. That some of the Lucky Starr books are more interesting than others has nothing to do with the audience for whom they were intended. Had Asimov given the concept of juvenile writing the careful thought that is so apparent in his other writing, he would have realized that the tag "juvenile" means much more than simple characters carrying out a simple plot with bits of action thrown in to keep the story going for the required hundred and fifty pages or so. Some of the best juvenile books have become classics that defy age group classification. Perhaps because the Lucky Starr books were not aimed at Asimov's usual readers—they were much simpler and far more action-oriented—Asimov's publishers attempted to sidestep any adverse fan reaction by the disclaimer, "juvenile." The most juvenile aspects of the series are the titles and the packaging.

This is not to say that all the Lucky Starr books will satisfy even the most devoted Asimov fan. Had *David Starr, The Pirates of the Asteroids,* and *The Big Sun of Mercury* actually been written by someone named Paul French, the likelihood is that they would be long forgotten. It's a safe bet that Asimov's name is the only thing that keeps them in print. Still, the entire series cannot be summarily dismissed. The description of underwater life is, in itself, sufficient reason for reading *The Oceans of Venus.* The final two books—*The Moons of Jupiter* and *The Rings of Saturn*—easily stand on their own, outdistancing the earlier books in conception, characterization, subtlety, and, simply, interest.

7

THE GODS THEMSELVES: A REALIZED VISION

"Against stupidity, the gods themselves contend in vain."
The Gods Themselves

The Gods Themselves is easily Asimov's best novel. He has often called it his favorite, and soon after its publication in 1972, it won him his first Nebula Award and later, a Hugo. Like "The Bicentennial Man" which came several years later, this novel, his first since 1958, began as a short story commissioned for a science fiction anthology, but grew well beyond its intended length.

Originally *The Gods Themselves* was supposed to be five thousand words long; after a week's work, its author had completed ten thousand words. It was the first time in thirteen years that "I felt the thrill of writing science fiction, I didn't want to stop, and I decided I wasn't going to. Let it go on to its natural length."

As in "Stranger in Paradise" and "The Bicentennial Man," Asimov once again affirms that intelligence is not solely human; but this time he suggests that no matter how great the intelligence, it will, in the face of all reason, succumb to expedience. Sparked by a quote from the Schiller drama *The Maid of Orleans*—"Against stupidity, the gods themselves contend in vain"—Asimov explores the idea that with intelligence, both human and inhuman, comes the potential for stupidity.

The story is divided into three distinct parts. The first takes place on Earth in the year 2100. Man's condition has been revolutionized by a source of cheap, nonpolluting energy. Beings from a parallel universe have discovered a way of exchanging matter with ours through a process known as the Electron Pump which supplies both universes with the energy they require. The Electron Pump creates energy only because the natural laws of the two universes are radically different; in the exchange of energy, however, these natural laws are being mixed. One of Earth's scientists, Peter Lamont, deduces that this mixing will, in time, cause our sun to explode, to become a supernova.

The Pump has made of Earth such a paradise that those responsible for Earth's well-being are unwilling even to consider Lamont's hypothesis as a possibility. Self-interest stands in the way of reason.

As the first section ends, Lamont despairs of the universal stupidity and of his own impotence in the face of it.

In the second section, Asimov shifts the reader to the parallel universe, an unearthly world as believable as any in science fiction. The only visible living beings inhabit caves beneath the planet's surface, venturing to the surface only to feed on sunlight—the food these creatures consume is energy. Their small society is divided into two classes of beings—Soft Ones and Hard Ones. Little is said about the Hard Ones, who resemble mysterious, god-like overseers. The Soft Ones are organized into families, called triads, with a "rightling" known as a Rational, a "leftling" Parental, and a "midling" Emotional.

Both the Rational and Parental take the male pronoun; only Emotionals are referred to as female. Distinctly different in appearance, the Rational is ovoid and fairly rigid, although in moments of excitement, he sometimes loses control and becomes irregularly shaped; the Parental is "blockish" and seems to become more so as he grows older;

the Emotional, according to creator Asimov, "in physical matter was apparently semigaseous" and can mix her atoms with those of any solid object, can sink into matter as solid as a rock. This property of the Emotional makes possible the triad's most important function—"melting." With the Rational on the left, the Parental on the right, and the Emotional in the middle, the three "melt" together, often for days at a time, for the dual purposes of propagation and pleasure in the parallel universe's equivalent of sexual intercourse.

Each of the three sexes also possesses distinctive personality traits which dictate their roles in the triad. The Rational is considered the leader of the family. The most intelligent member, he makes decisions about the welfare of the triad and spends a great deal of time away from the family studying with the Hard Ones. In general, Rationals are deferred to by members of the other two sexes and tend to be aloof, rarely exhibiting emotion.

The Parental, both mother and father, decides when to initiate children; he bears them, nurtures them, disciplines them, and makes all the decisions regarding their rearing. The Parental is truly single-minded and has few thoughts that are not connected with the welfare of the children. He has little life outside the family and leaves all other decision-making to the Rational.

The Emotional's nature is totally different from the other two. Her life seems to have no purpose except to act as the intermediary in melting. With no family duties and no inclination for intellectual pursuits, she spends most of her time with other Emotionals gossiping as they feed together on the planet's surface.

In creating a sexuality for this parallel universe among intelligences so dissimilar to ours, Asimov's imagination could have led him in any number of bizarre directions. Instead he chose to build on three common human sexuality stereotypes. The Rational follows the cold, logical, cerebral father figure of western civilization. The Emotional follows the generalized behavior patterns of the irrational female. Interestingly, Asimov chose the nurturing aspects of the maternal stereotype for his third sex, the Parental, implying that our nurturing instincts do not belong exclusively to either male or female—that while they can belong to one or both or neither, this instinct exists apart from sexuality.

The word stereotype normally has a pejorative connotation, but in *The Gods Themselves*, stereotypes are not used as shorthand to designate character. By using them as an essential element, Asimov is able to invest a totally alien environment with identifiable characteristics that add an emotional dimension to what might have been simply an imaginative intellectual creation.

In this parallel universe the stars are growing cold, and as a result, food is growing scarce. Fewer triads are able to initiate the children who will form new triads, and the population is dwindling. In search of new energy sources, these beings have contacted our universe and have set up the energy transfer system that, at their end, they call the Positron Pump.

The story revolves around an exceptional triad: Rational Odeen, Parental Tritt, and Emotional Dua.

Not only the most intelligent of all living Rationals and the Hard Ones' star pupil, rightling Odeen is also strongly drawn to the physical pleasure of melting and appreciates Dua's unusual characteristics even when they may be detrimental to the triad. Where other Rationals would be cold and objective, Odeen takes secret pride in Dua's eccentricities and seems to understand her longings. His actions are not strictly rational and out of a sense of sympathy with Dua, he often counsels Tritt to be patient with her.

Like all Parentals, Tritt is strongly dedicated to his children, but he can also be exceptionally bold and resourceful. He is capable of conceiving a complex plan and of taking independent action, in the process venturing far from his natural domain, the nursery.

Dua is the most unique member of the triad. She is an Emotional with a strange desire and capacity for intellectual growth. Unlike other Emotionals, she is a loner who often strays far away from Odeen and Tritt. Even in childhood she has never felt like other Emotionals. She detests the bovine activity of feeding that occupies most of their time. Oddly, she desires to learn, and as she matures, exhibits an uncharacteristic capacity for intellectual growth. At first she is indulgently encouraged by Odeen. But later, growing more rebellious and less satisfied with Odeen's patronizing explanations, she begins secretly to eavesdrop in the forbidden area of the Hard Ones.

Towards the end it is Dua who, like the scientist in the first section, discovers that the continued operation of the Pump will lead to the explosion of our sun. She, however, comes to realize that the destruction of the other universe will occur not through ignorance but through design. As long as Earth exists, the Pump can only operate with its cooperation. The Hard Ones, led by the mysterious Estwald, have decided that their best interests will be served if the sun does explode, thereby releasing huge quantities of energy that they can directly tap. Like Lamont in the first section, Dua becomes obsessed with stopping the Pump. She, too, fails but for a very different reason. The scientist is unable to overcome the shortsightedness of his superiors although it will lead to certain destruction of the universe. Dua, who finds her superiors, the Hard Ones, equally contemptible in their expedient acceptance of this destruction, learns to her horror that she cannot succeed.

As Odeen explains to Dua toward the end of this second section

> *The Soft Ones are immature forms of the Hard Ones.* We are first children as Soft Ones, then adults as Soft Ones, then Hard Ones. . . .
> . . . whenever we melt, whenever the triad melts, we become a

Hard One. The Hard One is three-in-one, which is why he is Hard. During the time of unconsciousness in melting we are a Hard One. But it is only temporary, and we can never remember the period afterwards. We can never stay a Hard One long; we must come back. But all through our life, we keep developing . . . there comes the possibility of the final stage, where the Rational's mind by itself, without the other two, can remember those flashes of Hard One existence. Then, and only then, he can guide a perfect melt that will form the Hard One forever, so that the triad can live a new and unified life of learning and intellect.

As Dua fades into that last "perfect melt," she can only cry, No, we can't stop Estwald. *We* are Estwald.

She and her two partners in the triad are indeed exceptional; they are Estwald, the Hard One who originally formulated the Machiavellian plan and engineered its realization.

In the final section, rationality does finally overcome stupidity but only because it is able to offer an equally expedient alternative. Here Asimov returns to our universe, moving the story from Earth to a well-established colony on the Moon. Benjamin Dennison, another disgruntled scientist, has discovered the validity of Peter Lamont's theory—the Electron Pump is upsetting the natural balance of our universe through its introduction of matter from the parallel universe. But Dennison's research into this theory reaches a dead end until he meets Selene Lindstrom.

As a result of genetic engineering, she possesses the power of "intuitionism." Beginning with Dennison's basic premise that "the number two is ridiculous and can't exist," they work together, she providing direction and insight, while he furnishes the ultimate scientific proof. Together they correctly reason that:

> It could make sense to suppose that our own Universe is the only one we live in and directly experience. Once, however, evidence arises that there is a second universe as well, the one we call the para-Universe, then it becomes absolutely ridiculous to suppose

that there are two and only two Universes. If a second Universe can exist, then an infinite number can. Between one and the infinite in cases such as these, there are no sensible numbers. Not only two, but any finite number, is ridiculous and can't exist.

The method that they develop for reaching these other universes can also correct the imbalance created by the Pump. Only when Dennison and Selene can offer this alternative as a *fait accompli* are Earth's leaders willing to consider, and finally agree, that the Electron Pump would have destroyed them.

Freed from the spectre of losing the comfortable life made possible by the Pump, Earth's leaders embrace the former pariahs, Dennison and Lamont, as heroes. For once, despite itself, stupidity has been overcome, but as Dennison points out, "there are no happy endings in history, only crisis points that pass."

The first and third sections of this novel are typically Asimovian in their recognizable view of a future society. The problems of this future society are really ours: while we know that our supply of energy is limited, we refuse to acknowledge that fact because acknowledgment would mean changing the quality of our lives. In Asimov's twenty-second century, they face a similar situation but cannot even allow themselves to consider that a problem exists. The culture of 2100 A.D. is very much like our own, and the differences that do exist, notably in lunar life, have recognizable roots in our present-day culture.

Both the first and third sections are good, serviceable science fiction. They speculate about an intriguing solution to the problem of energy production based on what seem to be reasonably scientific principles. At the same time, they offer a comment on a significant social problem—our willingness to accept technological solutions for the immediate relief they provide and to put off worrying about consequences for the future.

What takes *The Gods Themselves* out of the realm of the

serviceable and transforms it into the best work of one of America's major science fiction writers is the middle section of the book. But this middle section is much like Dua; it is only completely realized as part of a triad. It needs the frames provided by the opening and closing sections. The first is necessary if we are to understand the tragedy that unfolds in the second. The third offers a satisfying resolution without lessening the impact of the middle section.

Despite the familiar milieu of our universe, we hardly identify with the characters as people except on a purely cerebral level. But as soon as we enter the para-Universe and meet Dua, the novel takes on an emotional dimension much like that later created in "The Bicentennial Man."

This emotional dimension revolves around an unusual topic for Asimov, sexuality. Asimov claims in his autobiography that he took this direction because of an offhand comment by his editor at Doubleday.

> Larry had shown the first part to a paperback house and they had expressed interest, but had said, "Will Asimov be putting some sex into the book?"
>
> Larry said firmly, "No!"
>
> When Larry told me this I instantly felt contrary enough to want to put sex into the book. I rarely had sex in my stories and I rarely had extraterrestrial creatures in them either, and I knew there were not lacking those who thought that I did not include them because I lacked the imagination for it.
>
> I determined, therefore, to work up the best extraterrestrials that had ever been seen for the second part of my novel. There were not to be just human beings with antennae or pointed ears, but utterly inhuman objects in every way. And I determined to give them three sexes and to have that entire section of *The Gods Themselves* revolve about sex—*their* sex.

This was not an idle boast. On those few occasions in the past when he did write about sex, it was only in a perfunctory and often clumsy way. Ironically, it was only when he wrote about an unearthly world that he was able to communicate the deep emotional, physical, and even intellectual components of sexuality.

Every aspect of life in the para-Universe is in some way connected with sex. In this world "melting" shares many of the functions of human sexuality: it is the means of procreation, it provides great physical pleasure, it fosters intimacy, and yet is often a source of conflict among the partners.

But "melting" goes beyond this. During the act, the three partners *actually* become one, mixing their atoms, temporarily taking their mature form as a Hard One. And while they cannot recall these "flashes of Hard One existence," these periods of "melting" are responsible for the Rational's huge intuitive leaps that lead to his greatest intellectual insights. The act is also an integral part of their maturation process.

All this Asimov accomplishes naturally, without any of the convoluted exposition that mars some of his later stories. Skillfully he reveals the depth and pervasiveness of this sexuality, adding facets not merely as a contrivance to advance the story line but to enhance the illusion of reality. Dua often avoids sex with the other members of the triad because she fears that initiating a child will bring her closer to death. Instead she continues to indulge in the common practice of rock rubbing, secretly suspecting that other Emotionals do too. The two members of the triad to whom Asimov gives the male pronoun have a strong physical attraction for each other. Before Dua was introduced to complete the triad, Odeen and Tritt attempted "melting" without their midling Emotional, a practice, we are told, that is common among Parentals and Rationals. Even when the triad is complete, the strongest bond is between the two males, combining elements of friendship as well as sexual attraction.

Asimov avoids a graphic description of "melting," not out of prudery, but to underscore his point that neither the emotional component of life nor the intellectual is inherently human. He is interested in similarities, not differences, and had he been more explicit in his physical description of "melting," he would have driven a wedge between two intelligent life forms, forms with similar potential—for love as well as stupidity. A more visual description might have resulted in a story about monsters rather than about beings who achieve a luminous, yet recognizable reality.

As important as sexuality is to this second section, Asimov had no need to provide graphic illustration. He was not writing about physical gymnastics but about love as the prime element in the sex relationship.

Love seems an odd word to use as an emotion felt by unearthly creatures. Still, although no one talks about it—the word is hardly used—love is the element that unifies this section, and in his depiction of love, Asimov turns an interesting idea into superior fiction.

One of the disappointing aspects of the novel is that the love/sex relationship in the third section never rises to the level of the second. Asimov often approaches deep emotion directly, much in the way he narrates a story. We know that Selene and Dennison are attracted to each other because they tell us so. The plot requires that the words of desire be used, but the feeling behind them is absent. Here sexual attraction is depicted by suggestive banter between man and woman; love is a matter of jealous arguments and embarrassed looks. These emotions never spill over into the other aspects of their lives; the neat compartmentalization allows for none of the subtle characteristics that lend depth to the triad, a depth that is totally missing in the last third of the novel.

As sexuality pervades every aspect of life in the para-Universe, so does love pervade every aspect of the relationship among the members of the triad. It is not primarily a romantic love; nor is it sentimental. Odeen, Dua and Tritt are often annoyed, troubled, perplexed, even angered by one another. Just as often they are affectionate, sympathetic, and caring. There is more love evident in Dua's, "It's good to see you, Right-dear," than in any of the overt comments that pass between Selene and Dennison.

Asimov's portrayal of this most complex "human" experience that encompasses sexual desire, desire for procreation, tenderness, moral sustenance, and meaningful intelligence is an unqualified artistic success.

The purpose of art is to allow us to handle directly those facets of existence that do not yield to empirical study, and to see those facets as part of a whole. Most science fiction, the type Asimov calls "social science fiction," is interested in speculating about what might be, in exploring the various possibilities facing future societies. They are works that allow the intellect an unusual imaginative freedom. The perceptive exploration of personal relationships among realistically drawn, emotionally complex characters is normally considered the province of mainstream fiction. *The Gods Themselves* stands as Asimov's finest novel because he unifies disparate complex ideas and embodies them in a story that melds the best qualities of science fiction and mainstream fiction.

8

THE PROPERTIES OF INTELLIGENCE: THE LATE STORIES

"Your brain is man-made, the human brain is not. Your brain is
constructed, theirs developed. To any human being who is intent
on keeping up the barriers between himself and a robot, those
differences are a steel wall a mile high and a mile thick."

The Bicentennial Man and Other Stories

In Asimov's autobiography, he implies that by 1954 his
careers as a science fiction writer and university professor
were now dead ends; he felt that in these areas he had
probably achieved as much success as he ever would:

> I might do things that were better than *Nightfall, The Foundation
> Trilogy, I, Robot,* or *The Caves of Steel,* but surely not much better.
> They were already recognized as classics, and I had been writing
> for fifteen years and I had yet to make more than ten or eleven
> thousand dollars a year as a writer.
>
> I didn't see how I could ever do better than that, especially since
> there was bound to come a time soon when a newer and younger
> group of writers would take over and sweep myself and my con-
> temporaries from the field—as we had done to the writers of the
> 1930's.

But with America's burgeoning interest in the sciences
sparked by the launching of Sputnik, Asimov turned his
efforts towards popularizing scientific material.

He soon found that he enjoyed explaining phenomena
as diverse as the neutrino and the human brain in terms
intelligible to the layman. The response of this audience
was so positive that he turned almost exclusively to writing
non-fiction and today has published over 120 such works.

With the publication of the last book of the Lucky Starr

series, *The Rings of Saturn* in 1958, Asimov's science fiction output came to an almost complete halt. The only stories that he has written since then are ones that were commissioned by editors. Even his one science fiction novel written after 1958 began as a commissioned story.

Many of these later stories are eminently forgettable—they seem to be "armchair" stories where the entire plot consists of one character explaining something to another.

Yet despite the evidence presented by his slim output and the perfunctory quality of these lesser stories, Asimov must still be considered one of America's leading science fiction writers. On at least three occasions in the years following 1958, he has produced works of superior science fiction. One of these works, *The Gods Themselves*, would have justified its author's reputation as a major science fiction writer even if it were his only novel.

The common denominator in "Stranger in Paradise," "The Bicentennial Man" and *The Gods Themselves*, as well as many of the other late stories is the concept that intelligence may not be the sole property of the human being. We are in an era when humans find themselves competing less and less successfully with machines, when the abuses of our environment have increased our awareness of the importance of other life forms. Our claim to human superiority now rests on what we consider to be our unique intelligence. Asimov asks that we examine the properties of intelligence and explore the possibility that it may not be inherently human.

In the future world of "Stranger in Paradise," the intelligence that interests Asimov is that of an autistic child, an intelligence that does not fit in this world and forces the child to totally withdraw from it. For its part, the world terms him useless, and he is saved from euthanasia because a scientist is intrigued by his abnormality. Only when the autistic child's brain is introduced to an inhuman world does it find an environment hospitable to it.

The problem facing scientists in this story is the need for an Earthbound computer sophisticated enough to direct data-gathering robots on Mercury over fifty million miles away. The robot is easily adapted to the high temperatures and intense solar radiation, but in these prepositronic brain days, there is no computer complex enough to monitor every possible perception. The solution is to use a human brain, one not suited to life on our planet, and by giving it a robot's body adapt it to a radically different world.

Connected to the new body by radio signals, the brain of the autistic child senses that his robot body has landed on Mercury and for the first time in his life, he feels at home.

"He jumped, and rose slowly in the air with a freedom he had never felt, and jumped again when he landed, and ran, and jumped and ran again, with a body that responded perfectly to this glorious world, this paradise in which he found himself. A stranger so long and so lost—in paradise at last."

The intelligence here, though definitely human, is unable to function effectively in its natural earthly environment. Its fulfillment lies in following a nonhuman direction—in a metal body exploring a world where no man could survive.

"Stranger in Paradise" is not without serious flaws. Asimov sets the story in a society where it is an embarrassing oddity to have a sibling. Much time is spent in dealing with the difficulties that arise when two brothers accidentally come face to face. In *The Naked Sun*, Asimov creates a believable social order in which any close human contact is considered obscene. Here, however, his premise is never convincing. It never ceases to appear contrived and almost succeeds in obfuscating the part of the story that is significant and beautiful.

One step further along in Asimov's evaluation of intelligence and its inherent properties, "The Bicentennial

Man" deals with a man-made intelligence that one hesitates to call artificial.

Andrew Martin, whose positronic brain has been designed for general intelligence rather than to perform specialized tasks, is one of the early products of U.S. Robots and Mechanical Men. Purchased by the Martin family as a valet and butler, he is often prevented from carrying out his household tasks by the two Martin children who have discovered that they can order him to play. When one child orders Andrew to carve a piece of jewelry, the Martins discover that Andrew is an anomaly—he is able to create original works of art.

Soon Andrew is excused from all household duties and allowed to follow his own artistic inclinations. The money he earns is put into a trust fund for him. As Andrew is given more and more freedom, the Martins tend to treat him less and less like a robot—he is never given orders—and more like a member of the household. He is even given his own workshop, and when after thirty years, Andrew asks for his freedom, the Martins initiate an unprecedented court suit that leads to a monumental judicial decision: "There is no right to deny freedom to any object with a mind advanced enough to grasp the concept and desire the state."

After seventy years as an artist, Andrew turns his attention to history, specifically the history of robots. In conjunction with his new career, he wages another legal battle which leads to the first laws that protect robots from human aggression and humiliation. By now he has taken to wearing clothes, a move that seems appropriate despite his metal body.

U.S. Robots is far from pleased with Andrew's notoriety; in fact, his existence has changed the entire course of robotic development. They are embarrassed and even frightened by this man-made creation which has developed into both an artist and a social scientist. One hundred years after his creation, positronic brains are designed only for specific and limited uses.

When Andrew asks for an organic android body, one that would have the outward appearance of a man, his unusual status forces the scientists to acquiesce.

Andrew's new body also marks a new stage in his development—he begins to study the organic humanoid body and eventually becomes a pioneering authority on prosthetics. Ironically, as U.S. Robots moves away from individually brained units—a gigantic positronic brain now directs thousands of drones—human beings become more and more like Andrew Martin as his prosthetic devices are adopted to prolong their lives.

By his sesquicentennial, Andrew has become a well-known figure and can boast, "I have contributed artistically, literally, and scientifically to human culture as much as any human being now alive." At this point Andrew Martin reveals his life-long driving ambition—to become a human being.

For the next forty-nine years humans refuse to acknowledge the dissolution of the last remaining barrier between themselves and a form of intelligence which differs only in origin. As one character tells Andrew, humans believe they are superior because "Your brain is man-made, the human brain is not. Your brain is constructed, theirs developed."

While it is true that Andrew's brain was constructed, actual brain matter is not the true measure of intelligence. As Asimov shows so clearly in this story, all intelligence, whether its origins be organic or inorganic, must follow a process of development. Had Andrew been designed to perform only specific tasks, he would have been created with all the knowledge he would ever require. But knowledge is not intelligence and his intellectual capacity would have been static. There could have been no opportunity for any further development.

Andrew's positronic brain, however, is nonspecific; early in his life, he can be lured away from household duties, convinced that a child's order to play is more important.

As he is given the freedom to work as an artist, he discovers that these creative activities make the circuits of his brain "somehow flow more easily," a process that he equates with enjoyment.

Once begun, this process of intellectual development is irreversible. The creative artist must constantly make complex decisions, and soon Andrew is able to make a most unrobot-like decision, the decision to be free.

From this point forward Andrew's awareness grows exponentially until it can encompass not only creative intuition and deductive reasoning, but perhaps what is most important, emotion. Only at this advanced stage in his development is Andrew Martin capable of asking himself what it is that separates him from humans.

Nobody can supply this answer, not even the bitterest opponents to his campaign for humanity. Ultimately it is Andrew himself who discovers the root of human antipathy to his ultimate goal—he is immortal.

So Andrew arranges for an operation that will allow him to weaken and gradually die, an act that catches the imagination of the world. On his two hundreth anniversary, only days before his death, the world declares him the Bicentennial Man.

Andrew Martin's last decision represents the apex of his development. Asimov implies that Andrew's real achievement lies not in choosing mortality over immortality but in his ability to rise above his limitations. There are many examples of men and women who overcome severe physical and mental limitations in pursuit of an ideal—Beethoven composing his finest work after he was totally deaf, the crippled Renoir painting his canvasses with a brush attached to his hand, and in our own time, the unusual accomplishments of Helen Keller. As a robot, Andrew Martin must obey the Three Laws of Robotics, including the Third Law: every robot must protect its own existence. As a fully developed intelligent being, Andrew Martin can realize the implications of the highest human motivation—idealism. "I have chosen between the death of my body and the death of my aspirations and desires. To have let my body live at the cost of the greater death is what would have violated the Third Law."

The prospect of artificially created life is a frightening possibility to many people—perhaps because it threatens the notion that man is a singular creation. Even artificially created forms of intelligence—forms which modern computers are only now approaching—are often viewed with distaste as cold and inhuman machines. Science has yet to create a computer that can truly be called intelligent, yet whenever the possibility is even considered, it is most often depicted as a threat. In "The Bicentennial Man" Asimov suggests that the term inhuman may not be apt for true artificial intelligence. While he stops short of implying that one cannot have true intelligence without humanity, he makes the point that the quality of humanness can be a property of artificial intelligence. In the most sympathetic terms he explores the possibility that we may some day be capable of creating forms of intelligence that are not discernibly different from human intelligence.

Asimov asks those of us who may find this concept disquieting to consider another type of technology that will radically alter human life, perhaps in the near future. Will people consider themselves inhuman because their blood is pumped by a mechanical heart or because their retinas have been replaced by electronic sensors? When Andrew is told, ". . . however much you may be like a human being, you are *not* a human being," he asks: "In what way not? . . . I have the shape of a human being and organs equivalent to those of a human being. My organs, in fact, are identical to those in a prosthetized human being."

"The Bicentennial Man" is a simple, straightforward story that represents the mature Asimov at his best. In his earlier stories, emotions and characterizations are usually secondary to the development of plot and theme, often giving these stories a flat and puzzle-like quality. Although the theme of this story is as abstract and as significant as any he has ever attempted, Asimov allows the emotional content of his characters' lives to take center stage.

In the delineation of his best characters—Joseph Schwartz, the Mule, Elijah Baley—Asimov achieves a complexity of motivation that accounts in large part for their appeal. In a way this achievement is analogous to the cerebral mechanics of plot but with an added element—with the increase in the character's potential and unpredictability, the reader's attachment becomes emotional as well as intellectual.

Paradoxically, in a story centered around a mechanical being, it is emotion that dictates the plot. The story, while beautifully organized, is driven by Asimov's emotional, even tender vision of the character:

> Andrew's thoughts were slowly fading as he lay in bed.
> Desperately he seized at them. Man! He was a man! He wanted that to be his last thought. He wanted to dissolve—die—with that.

Although he began this as a commissioned story, it is easy to understand why "The Bicentennial Man" grew to twice its intended length and why Asimov says that it "had me almost in tears when I finished."

Conclusion

For Asimov the term science fiction is an appellation with two components—science and fiction. That he insisted on scientific accuracy may at times have kept him from fanciful conjecture, but at the same time it strengthened his fiction. Bound by his belief in and knowledge of science, he wrote about human characters and situations close to our own experience. The result is that futuristic hardware and exotic settings recede to the background. What shines through Asimov's work is the human quality that he is able to impart to aliens, semigaseous beings, even plants and machines.

Although Asimov admits to enjoying science fiction, he has been careful to point out that he takes it seriously—his work cannot be labeled escapist. In Asimov's fictional worlds, he has chosen themes that lose no validity when transferred to the future: artificial intelligence—its effects on society and society's effects on it; the uses and dangers of technology; the economic, political, religious forces behind the rise and fall of empires; the many manifestations of prejudice between races, species, men, and machines.

It is not mere coincidence that Asimov was writing at a time when science fiction outgrew its genre label and became a noteworthy component of contemporary fiction. Because his work is rooted in a recognizable reality, he is accessible to a wide and varied audience. The breadth of his appeal is still apparent today when even his earliest work not only remains in print but continues to attract new generations of readers.

In an age of specialization where the division between science and the arts is so sharply perceived, Asimov ignores the distinction by bringing the best of one to the other. To fiction he brings the rigorous investigations of science; to science he brings the unifying vision of fiction.

NOTES

(Unless the cloth edition is readily available, the paper edition has been cited.)

INTRODUCTION

1	"Science fiction is . . ."	Isaac Asimov, *Is Anyone There?* (Garden City, N.Y.: Doubleday & Co., 1967), p. 290.
4	"a literary man . . ."	Isaac Asimov, *In Memory Yet Green* (Garden City, N.Y.: Doubleday & Co., 1979), p. 205.
5	"It was a . . ."	Isaac Asimov, *Opus 100* (Boston: Houghton Mifflin Co., 1969), p. xiii.
5	"I have never . . ."	Ibid., p. xi.

CHAPTER 1

7	"Mankind will spread . . ."	Isaac Asimov, *The Martian Way and Other Stories* (New York: Fawcett Crest, 1955), p. 46.
7	"and in the . . ."	Isaac Asimov, *Buy Jupiter and Other Stories* (Garden City, N.Y.: Doubleday & Co., 1975), p. 113.
8	John W. Campbell . . .	*In Memory Yet Green*, p. 295.
8	"there came total . . ."	Isaac Asimov, *Nightfall and Other Stories* (Garden City, N.Y.: Doubleday & Co., 1969), p. 9.
9	"The testimony of . . ."	Ibid., p. 25.
9	"the tiny bit . . ."	Ibid., p. 21.
10	"Not Earth's feeble . . ."	Ibid., p. 35.
10	"happy ignorance that . . ."	*In Memory Yet Green*, p. 296

10	When Asimov received . . .	Ibid., p. 297, footnote.
11	"the most conspicuous . . ."	Ibid., p. 326.
11	"it has its . . ."	Isaac Asimov, *The Early Asimov* (Garden City, N.Y.: Doubleday & Co., 1972), p. 135.
11	"a tale about . . ."	*In Memory Yet Green*, p. 231.
14	"I sometimes got . . ."	*The Early Asimov*, pp. 191–92.
18	"with the patience . . ."	*Buy Jupiter*, p. 98.
19	"Dusty lumberyards with . . ."	*The Martian Way*, p. 125.
20	In the case . . .	Publisher Twayne Press folded before publishing the collection and the story was sold to *Astounding Science Fiction*. *In Memory Yet Green*, p. 687.
20	"simple-minded and . . ."	Ibid., p. 650.
22	"concerned with the . . ."	*Is Anyone There?* p. 286.
22	"social science fiction . . ."	Isaac Asimov in Majorie Mithoff Miller, "The Social Science Fiction of Isaac Asimov," in *Isaac Asimov*, eds. Joseph D. Olander and Martin Harry (New York: Taplinger Publishing Co., 1977), p. 14.
23	"that branch of . . ."	*Is Anyone There?*, p. 286.
23	"based on the . . ."	Ibid., p. 290.
24	"Not one of . . ."	*The Martian Way*, p. 122.

CHAPTER 2

27	"There was a . . ."	Isaac Asimov, *I, Robot* (Garden City, N.Y.: Doubleday & Co., 1963), p. 17.
27	"If, in future . . ."	Isaac Asimov, *The Rest of the Robots* (Garden City, N.Y.: Doubleday & Co., 1964), p. 43.
27	"machines designed by . . ."	Ibid., p. xiii.
28	Three Laws of . . .	*I, Robot*, p. 51.
30	"brain of platinum . . ."	*The Rest of the Robots*, p. 42.
31	"I, myself, exist . . ."	*I, Robot*, p. 63.
31	"Because I, a . . ."	Ibid., p. 72.
34	"such small unbalances . . ."	Ibid., p. 196.
34	"No machine may . . ."	Ibid., p. 216.
35	"It was always . . ."	Ibid., p. 218.
35	"For all time . . ."	Ibid., p. 218.
37	"no more than . . ."	*The Rest of the Robots*, p. 86.
37	"would, therefore, be . . ."	*I, Robot*, p. 108.
38	"Robots have no . . ."	*The Rest of the Robots*, pp. 108–09.
38	"For two hundred . . ."	Ibid., pp. 161–62.

CHAPTER 3

| 41 | "What is beauty . . ." | *The Rest of the Robots*, p. 327. |
| 41 | "Some sort of . . ." | Ibid., p. 165. |

42	"Each City ..."	Ibid., p. 181.
44	"There were the ..."	Ibid., pp. 177–78.
45	"it is customary ..."	Ibid., p. 184.
45	"What are we ..."	Ibid., pp. 326–27.
47	"He had an ..."	Ibid., p. 377.
48	"an observer from ..."	Ibid., p. 384.
50	"the walls about ..."	Ibid., p. 512.
50	"May I touch ..."	Ibid., p. 545–46.
51	"Solaria inside out"	Ibid., p. 551.
52	"courage to face ..."	Ibid., pp. 550–51.
52	"had left the ..."	Ibid., p. 553.
52	"In *The Caves* ..."	Ibid., p. 555.

CHAPTER 4

55	"the sum of ..."	Isaac Asimov, *Foundation* (Garden City, N.Y.: Doubleday & Co., 1951), p. 28
56	"Hari Seldon was ..."	Isaac Asimov, *Second Foundation* (Garden City, N.Y.: Doubleday & Co., 1953), p. vii.
58	"an island of ..."	*Foundation*, p. 75.
59	"the Foundation was ..."	Isaac Asimov, *Foundation and Empire* (Garden City, N.Y.: Doubleday & Co., 1952), p. viii.
60	"that human reactions ..."	*Foundation and Empire*, p. 208.
61	"To me, men's ..."	Ibid., p. 222.
62	"first successful, well-rounded ..."	*In Memory Yet Green*, p. 415.
64	"When you lost ..."	*Second Foundation*, p. 10.
65	Asimov had wanted to ...	*In Memory Yet Green*, p. 540.
65	"I disliked it ..."	Ibid., p. 545.
65	"each Foundation story ..."	p. 540.

CHAPTER 5

69	"To the rest ..."	*Pebble in the Sky* (New York: Fawcett Crest, 1950), p. 38.
70	"rots and dies"	Ibid., p. 147.
73	"six feet, two ..."	*The Stars, Like Dust* (New York, Fawcett Crest, 1951), p. 27.
73	"a smoldering girl ..."	Ibid., p. 41.
77	"rather sulkily"	*In Memory Yet Green*, p. 415.
77	"rapidly, more rapidly ..."	Ibid., p. 415.
77	"I had grown ..."	Ibid., p. 494.

CHAPTER 6

81	"You should have ..."	*David Starr, Space Ranger* (New York: New American Library, 1952), p. 93.
81	"ruin my stories ..."	*Opus 100*, p. 7.
83	"a companion in ..."	*David Starr, Space Ranger*, p. 96.

| 83 | "pedestrian" | *In Memory Yet Green*, p. 654. |
| 83 | "If I had . . ." | *Lucky Starr and the Pirates of the Asteroids* (Greenwich, Conn.: Fawcett Books, 1953), p. 8. |

CHAPTER 7

89	"Against stupidity, the . . ."	Isaac Asimov, *In Joy Still Felt* (Garden City, N.Y.: Doubleday & Co., 1980) p. 554.
89	"I felt the . . ."	Ibid., p. 554.
91	"in physical matter . . ."	Ibid., p. 571.
93	"The Soft Ones . . ."	Isaac Asimov, *The Gods Themselves* (Garden City, N.Y.: Doubleday & Co., 1972), pp. 166–67.
94	"No, we can't . . ."	Ibid., p. 168.
94	"the number two . . ."	Ibid., p. 236.
94	"It could make . . ."	Ibid., p. 237.
95	"there are no . . ."	Ibid., p. 287.
96	"Larry had shown . . ."	*In Joy Still Felt*, p. 567.
99	"It's good to . . ."	*The Gods Themselves*, p. 133.

CHAPTER 8

101	"Your brain is . . ."	*The Bicentennial Man and Other Stories* (Garden City, N.Y.: Doubleday & Co., 1976), p. 169.
101	"I might do . . ."	*In Memory Yet Green*, pp. 707–08.
103	"He jumped, and . . ."	Ibid., p. 112.
104	"There is no . . ."	Ibid., p. 144.
105	"I have contributed . . ."	Ibid., p. 165.
106	"somehow flow more . . ."	Ibid., p. 138.
107	"I have chosen . . ."	Ibid., p. 171.
107	"however much you . . ."	Ibid., p. 165.
108	"Andrew's thoughts were . . ."	Ibid., p. 172.
108	"had me almost . . ."	*In Joy Still Felt*, p. 702.

BIBLIOGRAPHY

I. ISAAC ASIMOV'S SCIENCE FICTION

A. Novels

The Caves of Steel. Garden City, N.Y.: Doubleday & Co., 1964.

The Currents of Space. Greenwich, Conn., Fawcett Books, 1952.

David Starr, Space Ranger. New York: New American Library, 1952.

The End of Eternity. Greenwich, Conn.: Fawcett Publications, 1955.

Fantastic Voyage. New York: Houghton Mifflin, 1966.

Foundation. Garden City, N.Y.: Doubleday & Co., 1951.

Foundation and Empire. Garden City, N.Y.: Doubleday & Co., 1952.

The Gods Themselves. Garden City, N.Y.: Doubleday & Co., 1972.

Lucky Starr and the Big Sun of Mercury. New York: Fawcett Crest, 1956.

Lucky Starr and the Moons of Jupiter. New York: New American Library, 1957.

Lucky Starr and the Oceans of Venus. New York: Fawcett Crest, 1954.

Lucky Starr and the Pirates of the Asteroids. Greenwich, Conn.: Fawcett Books, 1953.

Lucky Starr and the Rings of Saturn. Greenwich, Conn.: Fawcett Books,.1958.

The Naked Sun. Greenwich, Conn.: Fawcett Publications, 1956.

Pebble in the Sky. New York: Fawcett Crest, 1950.

The Stars, Like Dust. New York: Fawcett Crest, 1951.

Second Foundation. Garden City, N.Y.: Doubleday & Co., 1953.

B. Short Story and Essay Collections:

Asimov's Mysteries. Garden City, N.Y.: Doubleday & Co., 1958.

The Best of Isaac Asimov. Garden City, N.Y.: Doubleday & Co., 1974.

The Bicentennial Man and Other Stories. Garden City, N.Y.: Doubleday & Co., 1976.

Buy Jupiter and Other Stories. Garden City, N.Y.: Doubleday & Co., 1975.

The Early Asimov. Garden City, N.Y.: Doubleday & Co., 1972.

Earth Is Room Enough. Garden City, N.Y.: Doubleday & Co., 1957.

I, Robot. Garden City, N.Y.: Doubleday & Co., 1963.

Is Anyone There? Garden City, N.Y.: Doubleday & Co., 1967.

The Martian Way and Other Stories. New York: Fawcett Crest, 1955.

Nightfall and Other Stories. Garden City, N.Y.: Doubleday & Co., 1969.

Nine Tomorrows. New York: Fawcett Crest, 1959.

Of Time and Space and Other Things. Garden City, N.Y.: Doubleday & Co., 1965.

Opus 100. Boston: Houghton Mifflin Co., 1969.

The Rest of the Robots. Garden City, N.Y.: Doubleday & Co., 1964.

C. Short Story Collections Edited by Asimov:

Before the Golden Age. Garden City, N.Y.: Doubleday & Co., 1974.

The Hugo Winners. Garden City, N.Y.: Doubleday & Co., 1962.

—. *Vol. Two.* Garden City, N.Y.: Doubleday & Co., 1971.

—. *Vol. Three.* Garden City, N.Y.: Doubleday & Co., 1977.

Nebula Award Stories Eight. New York: Harper & Row, 1973.

II. BIOGRAPHY AND CRITICISM

Asimov, Isaac. *In Joy Still Felt.* Garden City, N.Y.: Doubleday & Co., 1980.

—. *In Memory Yet Green.* Garden City, N.Y.: Doubleday & Co., 1979.

Fiedler, Jean, and Jim Mele, "Asimov's Robots." In *Critical Encounters,* edited by Dick Riley. New York: Frederick Ungar Publishing Co., 1978.

Silverberg, Robert, ed. *Galactic Dreamers, Science Fiction as Visionary Literature.* New York: Random House, 1977.

Olander, Joseph D., and Martin Harry Greenberg, eds. *Isaac Asimov.* New York: Taplinger Publishing Co., 1977.

Scithers, George, ed. *Isaac Asimov's Worlds of Science Fiction.* New York: Davis Publications, 1980.

Patrouch, Joseph F., Jr. *The Science Fiction of Isaac Asimov.* Garden City, N.Y.: Doubleday & Co., 1974.

INDEX